The Economics of Web Comics, 2ⁿᵈ Edition

A Study in Converting Content into Revenue

D1481457

The Economics of Web Comics
2nd Edition

A Study in Converting Content into Revenue

Todd Allen

Table of Contents

Introduction

February 10, 2007

All of a sudden, web comics are a hot topic, aren't they? In October, Saheli Datta, a reporter from *Business 2.0,* made a number of phone calls to people involved with web comics, asking questions from a financial perspective. You may not have seen the article, and that may be because it's been put on hold.

DC Comics is arguably the biggest technological laggard among the top print publishers. My understanding is that, when *Business 2.0* asked DC about their online plans, DC reported they were going to be launching an online initiative in December 2006. Well, obviously that didn't happen, and *Business 2.0* would appear to be waiting to see what the launch looks like, but we are now in an environment where the traditional publishers of print comics appear to be sprinting toward real online initiatives. A little more than fashionably late to the party, DC and Marvel could be missing out on a payday of up to $4 million per year by not jumping on the bandwagon.

That's right, four million dollars. How do I get to that number? If you skip ahead to Chapter 6A, you'll find some numbers and average prices for some of the early efforts in paid downloads of printed comics. Current market conditions seem to indicate 1% to 2.5% of the print sales levels as a target for a paid download. One online retailer in an industry with historical ties to comics and the comic book demographic reports 11% of their business coming from digital downloads. Prices in download efforts have ranged from $0.69 to full cover price. If you take ICV2.com's sales estimates for the direct market for December 2006 and plug those numbers and multiply out for a full year, you get some interesting results:

For a $0.99 download in the 1% - 2% of print circulation conversion range: $355,148 (DC circulation, 1%) to $747,203 (Marvel circulation, 2%)

At a possible mature market rate of 11%, Marvel's download revenues would project to $4,109,618 and DC's a bit over $3.9 million.

And that doesn't' even factor in merchandising revenue from direct to consumer offerings that neither publisher is currently pursuing (unless you're in the UK, where Marvel.co.uk is e-commerce enabled).

No, there's money in web comics.

This second edition updates and replaces *Online Comics Vs. Printed Comics: A Study in E-Commerce and the Comparative Economies of Content.* Updated chapters are signified by a letter after the chapter number, as we take a fresh look at topics like paid downloads, web comics in print and advertising.

Web comics aren't just about paid downloads and this book examines how both the individual cartoonist and publishing company can harness the web as revenue-generating medium and as an alternative to shrinking circulation of the direct comic market and limited opportunities in syndicated newspaper strips.

Chapter 1 – Context for Online Content

In the past decade, the relationship between printed content and Internet-based content has been an important topic in the communities of business, publishing and new media. Newspapers have seen their circulations decline and attribute part of that erosion to the World Wide Web, even as they profit by converting their classified sections to be searchable online, as much out of fear of eBay and Monster.com as for the additional revenue stream. Book publishers have introduced eBooks to varying degrees of success. Magazines, as well as newspapers, contemplate decisions of how much content, if any, to make freely available, and what to make available only by subscription. These entities struggle with the types of revenue models available to them: banner advertising (the digital equivalent of display advertising), subscriptions, pay-per-view, micropayments and affiliate programs.

In their seminal e-business book, *Blown to Bits*, Philip Evans and Thomas S. Wurster argue that emerging technology, especially of the Internet variety, can change the way businesses operate and destroy, or "blow up," a company's traditional value proposition. Their most quoted example is Encyclopedia Britannica, a once-proud publisher that ignored the emergence of new media and is now a shadow of its former self.

Indeed, online content and its business implications may well be too large a topic to address in a single exploration. With this in mind, consider the comic book. An invention of the early 1930s and a spin-off of the slightly older newspaper comic strip, it is considered by many, along with Jazz, to be an art form native to the United States. As with many forms of traditional printed content, the comic book industry has seen its fortunes ebb in recent years. At the same time, as some traditional publishers make exploratory, often abortive, initiatives into the world of online content, upstart cartoonists and, in some cases, web publishers are embracing the Internet.

The interplay between print and web comics is a microcosm for the relationship between print and online content. While the industry does have a certain number of issues unique unto itself, many of the lessons learned studying this relationship can be applied to the overall business of online content and the relationship between print and web.

This book will address issues of the comparative value of online revenue models, how online revenue compares to print revenue, when print or online formats are more advantageous and what the audience implications of format choices are, as well as providing a functional view of the business models and development of the formats.

Additionally, this book will examine the notion of whether online comics could wreck the economy of print comics, much like downfall and readjustment of Encyclopedia Britannica and the "Blown to Bits" scenario.

For those viewing this book in an academic light, this study is a capsule of print and online industries through February of 2004.

For those viewing this book as a study of business methods, consider that content is still content and there have been a finite number of ways used to monetize that content. Online comics represent a greater challenge than text-based websites, owing to the greater amount of bandwidth taken up by their images. Conversely, their bandwidth bill is inexpensive where compared to the cost of streaming audio or video content. The methods examined here are re-applicable to other types of content.

Chapter 2 – An Introduction to Print Comic Books, Their Economics, and Fall from Circulation Grace.

Comic books initially began as a subset of magazines in the 1930s, enjoying the same newsstand distribution channels utilized over the years as publications like *Time* or *Life*. Starting in the 1970s, an alternative market, aimed more at collectors, emerged. Referred to as the "direct market," this distribution channel offered its own unique set of economics. Whereas most magazines are displayed at newsstands and returnable if they do not sell, products in this direct market are offered at a higher discount (commonly 60% is offered to the distributor and between 40% - 55% to the retailer, dependent on volume) and are not returnable. This lack of returns made the direct market extremely efficient from an economic perspective and has allowed new and smaller publishers to enter into the market.

Starting in the mid-1980s, in addition to being the primary distribution outlet for these new or "independent" publishers, the direct market began to take on a greater over-all percentage of comic book sales for the traditional publishers, who started to see a decline in the number of newsstands carrying their product. By the mid-90s, this direct market had become the primary channel of distribution for all comics, with many titles from even the traditional publishers having no editions carried in the traditional magazine distribution system.

Traditional publishers, having originated on the newsstands and grown a direct market presence, would include Archie Comics, DC Comics, and Marvel Comics. Independent publishers, who originated in the direct market, would include Dark Horse Comics and Image

Comics, both of whom eventually ascended to the first tier of the remnants of the industry. Independent publishers still publishing today, while not being defined as "premiere" by Diamond, the current main distributor for the market, include Crossgen Comics, Oni Press, and Avatar Press. Some notable independent publishers that sprouted in the 1980's and 1990's, but eventually went out of business after some initial notoriety, include Eclipse Comics, First Comics, Comico, Chaos Comics, and Valiant Comics.

It is useful to look at sales levels of popular comic books of a given era, in order to better understand how drastically circulations have fallen in recent times. While hard sales numbers for early comic books are difficult to come by, it is commonly believed that in the 1940s, popular titles like *Superman* and *Captain Marvel* routinely sold in the neighborhood of one million copies per issue. Through the use of circulation auditing records, <u>The Standard Catalog of Comic Books</u> lists a circulation peaking at 530,824 for the September 1937 issue of *Famous Funnies*, the first modern comic book, whose circulation dropped to 319,000 by early 1940 (Miller 474). In roughly the same time period, *Tip Top Comics* is shown to range from 269, 938 to 441,618 copies per issue (Miller 1271) and *Feature Funnies / Comics* ranged from 221,982 to 387,914 copies per issue.

While 1940s and 1950 circulation records are not readily available, postal circulation statements indicate in 1960, *Superman* averaged 810,000 copies per month (Miller 1201), *Batman* sold 502,000 copies per month (Miller 170), and *The Flash*, sold 298,000 copies per month (Miller 506).

Jumping ahead to 1970, *Superman* was still a top seller with 446,678 for an average monthly circulation (Miller 1201). A younger comic, *The Amazing Spider-Man* averaged 322,195 (Miller 89) and *Batman* averaged 293,897 copies per month (Miller 171). In sharp contrast with modern times, *Archie* topped all superhero books with a 482,945 average copies per moth (Miller 116). Moving ahead to 1980, the transition to the direct market was slowly beginning, and the newsstand system had begun to wane. *The Amazing Spider-Man* averaged a monthly circulation of 296,712 (Miller 92), *Star Wars*, in the wake of the release of the second film in the first trilogy, averaged 255,985 copies (Miller 1165), and the *Fantastic Four* averaged 243,786 copies per month (Miller 481).

In 1992, the direct market was arguably at the height of its prowess. The "X-Men" franchise, which was just starting to gain popularity in the early '80s, had strong showings with 2 titles: *X-Men* with a staggering 967,808 copies per issue average (Miller 1419) and *Uncanny X-Men* at a level of 731,425 copies per month (Miller 1307). *The Amazing Spider-Man* even managed 544,000 copies each month (Miller 96). Unfortunately, accurate statistics are not available for the launch of Image Comics, a publisher made up of popular artists who broke away from Marvel to start their own company. It is believed that the first issues of several of their titles sold in the general area of 700,000 to one million copies, and these books were exclusive to the direct market. In 1992, all was good in the world of comic books, except perhaps with Archie. That publisher, which has never been a large player in the direct market system, still relied primarily on traditional magazine distribution methods. Their flagship book, *Archie*, had dropped to an average monthly circulation of

47,530 in 1992 (Miller 117). This was to be a sign of what lay ahead.

Sales started to dip in the direct market in the mid-'90s, and Marvel made a brief attempt to distribute their own books to the direct market in 1995. By 1996, the result of a major player removing itself from the market was a consolidation of distributors, with Diamond Comic Distributors emerging as the last major distributor after signing exclusivity deals with the remaining large publishers and purchasing their last major rival, Capital City Distribution (Miller 18).

1993 started a cooling off period for comic sales. In a normal market, demand would peak and then come back down to a consistent level. Instead of flattening out, the dip has continued for 10 years, although there have been signs of a flattening out in the last year: that is still a matter of debate in the industry.

Exacerbating the dip in sales has been the attrition of direct market retail outlets.

"In 1992, there were about 10,000 retail specialty shops that made up what we called The Direct Market. They purchased inventory from distributors and publishers on a non-returnable basis, a dramatic departure from traditional newsstand sales, and their primary product line was comics and comics-related merchandise," explains Tony Panaccio, the former Vice President of Product Development for Crossgen Entertainment, which was the fourth-largest direct market comic book publisher encountering before financial difficulties in 2003. "Today, that number is dramatically lower, and somewhat in dispute. Promoters of the industry claim that there are as many as 3,500 in operation today. After three years of continuous canvassing, via phone, Internet and direct in-person contact, my marketing department at CrossGen was able to ascertain the existence of only a little more than 2,000 such direct market specialty shops for comics last year" (Private Interview).

Bill Jemas, current Chief Marketing Officer and former President of Publishing and New Media for Marvel Comics, reports approximately 3000 retailers doing business with Marvel, but was unsure how many of those retailers had store fronts, which could account for some of the discrepancy between the two figures (Private Interview).

2003 finds the comic book industry locked into a direct market that has lost between 2/3 and 4/5 of its peak number of outlets, depending on which estimate is to be believed. Either is a staggering drop-off. At the same time, the traditional newsstand outlets have been largely abandoned.

Examining Business of Performing Audits International's (BPA) "Circulation Statement for the 6 Month Period Ended June 2003" for Marvel Comics, several interesting things come to light. First, in the breakout for May 2003, the Total Qualified Circulation is 3,095,661 copies. Of that number, only 131,625 are "Single Issue Sales," or newsstand-distributed copies. If May is representative of Marvel's circulation, and there is no reason to believe otherwise, then only 4.25% of Marvel's circulation comes from the traditional newsstand distribution system. Subscriptions, as a percentage of the monthly average circulation, only account for 3.3%. Thus, it becomes obvious that Marvel has moved beyond the traditional magazine distribution system, with less than 10% of their circulation coming through those channels. Going back to the May 2003 breakout, of the 47 titles published that month, only 23 had Single Issue Sales, meaning that slightly over half of the product line was only available through the direct market. Allowing for multiple issues published in that same month, as the monthly records account for total issues of a title in a given month, not per issue, this gives Marvel 6 titles over 100,000 in circulation, with the largest circulation being 163,000 copies to the inaugural issue of a re-launching of *Wolverine*. It should be noted that first issues of a title always get higher sales. It is somewhat difficult to tell the exact monthly circulations from the audit form, given Marvel's sporadic tendencies to ship multiple issues in random months, but it appears if you remove the Spider-Man movie adaptation's 2.5 million copies which was a promotional give-away with Wal-Mart, and remove two special 25-cent promotional comics, that the May issue of *Wolverine* was the best-selling issue of that six month period and the best selling comic books are clustered around 110-123,000 copies per month. A far cry from even where the market dipped in 1980.

The exact opposite of Marvel for the first half of 2003 is Archie Comics, whose "Archie's Plus Group" BPA circulation report for the same time period reveals 3.5% of their circulation coming from subscriptions, which roughly matches Marvel; however, 88% of their circulation comes from Single Issue Sales. Interestingly, their regular-sized comic books have very low circulations, with only one reaching 25,000 in average sales. Their digests, on the other hand sell very well, with two of them averaging 121,000 copies per month in that period, which would place them in the top 10, if not top 5 sellers at Marvel. It should be noted that the Archie Digests are usually placed in the checkout lanes of grocery stores, a highly coveted merchandise placement, and this most likely partially accounts for their superlative sales, comparative to the current market.

While the sales of those digests, regardless of the influence of point of purchase placement, indicate some possible viability, the standard format comic book seems to be almost an after-thought in the world of the newsstand. With the number of direct market outlets also having shrunk, this should be a point of concern.

When Jemas arrived at Marvel in 1999, newsstand sales were at 14%, according to the BPA's audits for the first half of the year, and the company made a conscious decision to walk away from the newsstand in favor of reprint collections in bookstores, owing to the serialized nature of the stories. "I have a pretty good imagination, but I can't see a twelve-year-old going to a newsstand six months in a row to pick up the right Spider-Man comic to get a complete story. I can see a twelve-year-old going to a bookstore and picking up a book with the whole Spider-Man story in it," is how Jemas explains the decision.

Also factoring in the decision to walk away from the newsstand was the limited ability to audit the returns and verify the return rate; the added expense of returns; and the lack of direct interaction with the newsstands, as opposed to the interaction with direct market retailers. Jemas does cite a successful newsstand distribution program in Waldenbooks stores implemented through Ingram (traditionally a distributor of books, not of magazines) where the comics are racked in a spinner near the magazine section and there is greater communication with the retailer, in terms of display and feedback.

On the subject of low subscription numbers, Jemas described subscriptions as a function of customer loyalty and as a lifestyle decision. By this definition, the majority of loyal customers would journey to a direct market retail outlet to buy comics. Marvel feels the direct market channel is more beneficial to them than subscriptions since it stresses loyalty in the form of a weekly pilgrimage to purchase the product. Jemas states that one of the reasons behind Marvel's policy of not over-printing comic books for potential retailer re-orders was to reinforce the habit of weekly purchases by the end consumer (Private Interview).

The above circulation numbers indicate the shrinking done to the top publishers, but do not show what has become of the independent publishers. Diamond Comics Distributors has 5 "Premiere Partners" whose products run in expanded listings in the front of the catalog. These "partners" are four comic book publishers: DC, Marvel, Image and Dark Horse; as well as Wizard, a popular magazine about comic books that occasionally publishes comic books under the "Black Bull" imprint. All other publishers are placed in the back of the catalog, which Panaccio describes as "cluttered, disorganized, and lacks any kind of organization. That's not by accident. It's by design."

"It is my belief – and I am not alone in this belief, but I am sure that many of my colleagues feel it is not in their best interests to voice their opinions on this matter – that the Department of Justice blew it when they initially investigated Diamond to examine its compliance with the anti-trust laws on the books right now," Panaccio said. "While many analysts within the DOJ could see the argument for technical compliance, especially when it is presented solely by Diamond's lawyers, I believe that any sitting judge would have seen through Diamond's definitions of 'broker' and 'distributor' in relation to their vendors, and ruled that Diamond was indeed in violation of anti-trust laws. In my mind, Diamond is one of the worst-case scenarios of monopoly in American publishing, and the resulting power and influence wielded by Diamond in the marketplace is unfair and illegal. It is fundamentally unjust that this criminal conduct is allowed to continue while thousands of retailers, thousands of creators and dozens of publishers locked outside the premier vendor club suffer under a system that was constructed solely for the purpose of entrenching and rewarding a select minority."

"Let's look at exactly what Diamond does for a moment," Panaccio explains. "1) They print a catalog, which they make outrageous money on. That catalog costs them about $1 per unit to make. They sell it to consumers for $5 per unit, and make an average of $5,000 per display ad, with more than 150 pages of display ads per issue. 2) They take big boxes and make them into little boxes and ship them, via UPS, which costs them very little. That's it -- there are, perhaps, four field sales reps, a few sales executives in Baltimore, and that's it. For an entire industry.

"Now -- if your main business is boxing and shipping, your margins are reduced with each new publisher that enters the market, and with each new store that opens. If 75 percent of all your product comes from 5 vendors, and the other 25 percent comes from a combination of 40 vendors, your margins actually rise when some of those other 40 vendors go bye-bye. If 75 percent of all the product you ship goes to 750 locations, and the other 25 percent goes to the remaining 2,400 locations, then your margins actually rise when those bottom feeder stores go bye-bye. Fewer vendors and fewer shipping points equals a higher margin of the product you are guaranteed to place no matter what, because you are a monopoly and have no competition.

"Diamond's primary business model is to shrink the comics industry down to its lowest common denominators and squeeze out any potential competition for its premier publishers" (Private Interview).

This view may be an extreme one, but keeping it in mind while viewing the Diamond sales chart indicates there is at least circumstantial evidence to take this viewpoint seriously.

ICV2 is a website for direct market and pop culture retailers run by the former owners of Capital City Distribution. Each month they issue estimated sales figures for the comic books Diamond distributes. While these numbers are estimates, they are commonly accepted in the industry as such, and can likely be considered accurate within 10%. Looking at the estimates for December 2003 (http://www.icv2.com/articles/home/4107.html), the bestselling independent comic (that is to say, from a company not listed in the front of the catalog) is Dreamwave's *TRANSFORMERS GENERATION ONE VOL 3 #0* at number 29 with an estimated 53,081 copies ordered. This may be slightly misleading as Dreamwave was formerly a studio distributed by Image Comics, the Transformers franchise was initially published through Image Comics, and the company was also engaging with a cross-over event with the "G.I. Joe" franchise, which was also being published by Image.

The next highest selling independent comic book is *MICHAEL TURNER PRESENTS ASPEN #3*, at number 71 with 27,864 estimated copies ordered. Again, Turner is a popular artist who recently left Image Comics and that comic features his "Fathom" character, who headlined a popular comic for Image.

The first independent comic not strongly associated with Image by both creative team and characters or a possible ownership arrangement with Diamond is *DARK DAYS #6* from IDW at 116 and with an estimated 18,536 copies ordered. So a truly independent book does not rank within the top 100 comic books ordered. *El Cazador*, the most popular title from Crossgen, is estimated at just under 18,000 copies, and more independent books start to show up after this.

Still, these are color books, and the independent publishers, particularly the self-publishers that popularized the direct market in the 1980s and 1990s, used to publish in black and white. This is the format from which the now famous "Teenage Mutant Ninja Turtles" came. The highest selling independent black and white comic book is *Knights of the Dinner Table #86*, the 201st most ordered comic book for December 2003 with an estimated 6,304 copies requested. Other top selling black and white independents include *Cerebus #297* estimated at 6,194 and *Queen & Country #22* estimated at 6,139 copies.

Perhaps a better demonstration of this phenomenon is the sales drop of *G.I. Joe*. *G.I. Joe* was licensed by the art studio, "Devil's Due," and published through Diamond premiere partner, Image Comics. The orders for the title in October, as estimated by ICV2, were 36,662 copies, 38,849 in November, and 36,300 in November, all under the Image banner. In January 2004, Devil's Due withdrew from their relationship with Image and published the book under their own name. January sales were estimated at

31,417, a 13.45% drop off from numbers that had been somewhat consistent over the previous quarter, despite continuous numbering on the title.

In fairness, two major publishers, Image and Dark Horse, do have some black and white titles with more of an independent flair, but these, on the whole, still tend to sell better than the true independents. Be it brand equity or catalog placement, there is a demonstrable reality that an independent publisher in the direct market is at a disadvantage.

Panaccio, again, has an apocalyptic anecdote about independent status and the Diamond system: "[At one point Crossgen was outselling premiere partner Dark Horse in both unit and dollar share.] We were doing with 15 titles what they couldn't do with 24 (mini-series included). Now, Crossgen expanded too fast, and cannibalized its own product line unit sales, which led to a greater market share but lower per-title unit sales. The imaginary golden calf was supposed to be that at 5 percent market share, Diamond would award CG premier status. That never came to be, for a number of reasons. The arbitrary limits are imposed by Diamond at Diamond's sole discretion. Keep in mind, Diamond acts on the behalf of their premier publishers. If a small publisher starts cutting into marketshare for the big five, it's usually not long after that the new publisher hits a wall, and has to retreat or reorganize."

While not citing Diamond as a problem, Jemas agrees that the direct market is no place for a new publisher to be successful. "It's not a business," is how Jemas phrases the proposition, citing the history of failed companies and poor margins on a print run of 10,000, the most he could imagine a newcomer to be able to sell. Jemas feels that

23

while you might not necessarily lose money, not enough profit margin is available to consider it more than hobby, if implemented on a small scale. ICV2's estimates of direct market sales would back up his assessment of sales potential, as well.

Another concern for the direct market is that of its continuing contraction. It is uncertain how many more direct market retailers will close. It is also uncertain at what point there would not be enough commercial outlets open to support the publishers participating in this market. Likely, as they are already squeezed to the bottom of the sales charts, independent publishers would likely be the first to go.

In summary, the printed comic book market has all but abandoned the newsstand, seen tremendous contraction in the available number of retail outlets for its new distribution system, seen its sales plummet and is plagued by conspiratorial theories with at least circumstantial supporting evidence of the distribution agent holding down smaller publishers.

Chapter 3: A Short History of Web Comics

Web comics started at much the same time that the direct market for print comics passed its peak and started the long slide. On September 23, 1993, Doctor Fun, the first regularly updated comic on the World Web Web was launched (What's New). This was a single panel cartoon in the tradition of "The Far Side," and still continues to be produced at: http://www.ibiblio.org/Dave/drfun.html.

As the web's popularity grew more comics gradually appeared online. From 1993 to 1997 saw the initial experimentation of web comics occur. Notable web comics include:

- In June 1995, Charley Parker launched the popular "Argon Zark" feature, which might be best described as an interactive comic book (Parker).
- "Kevin and Kell," launched in September 1995 by Bill Holbrook, who also creates two comic strips, "On the Fast Track" and "Safe Havens," for newspapers.
- Peter Zale started work on "Helen, Sweetheart of the Internet," in 1996. In 2000, it ceased to be a web comic strip and became a syndicated newspaper strip (Zale).

In 1997, as Diamond settled in as the primary point of comics distribution for the direct market and publishers became used to the section of their catalog, many currently popular strips started to appear. "Goats" first appeared on April 1, 1997 (Johnson). "Sluggy Freelance" first appeared on August 25, 1997. "User Friendly" first appeared on November 17, 1997 (Abrams).

After 1997, the flood gates were thrown open and the number of web comics proliferated quickly, with new strips each year and growing readerships. In all likelihood, part of the timing of the progression of web comics was due to circumstance of the technology distributing itself among the masses, but it still parallels the decline of the direct market and it is, at worst, an interesting coincidence that big wave of superstar strips started up as a shift in distributors tightened the clamp on independent comic books.

While there is not a wealth of historical audience data for the popularity of these web comics, it is possible to get a sense of the current traffic on these sites. "Penny Arcade," the most popular individual strip online reports an audience of 3.1 million readers and 29 million pageviews per month (Audience). Keenspot, a publisher of more than 50 web comics and a web comics portal unto itself, reports an audience of 2.5 million unique monthly visitor and a staggering 70 million pageviews per month. (Keenspot.com: Media Kit – What We Are) "Our most popular strip does well over 5 million," reports Darren "Gav" Bleuel, Keenspot co-owner and ad rep. "There are about 15 that do over a million--about five or six of those do over 2 million" (Bleuel). "Sinfest," Keenspot's most popular strip, links to a traffic tracking webpage that lists it as having 941,654 unique visitors in January 2004 ("Extreme Tracking – Sinfest"). In January 2003, "PVP" reported 9,714,513 pageviews and 449,882 unique visits (Kurtz, "Become a PVP Sponsor"). The risqué sex farce "Sexy Losers" reports 6 million pageviews per month and one million unique users ("Bald Rocket"). "Real Life" reports 5 million pageviews per month and 40,000 readers daily ("Real Life – Advertisers"). "Goats," arguably the first of the modern wave of web comics, reports 95,000 unique I.P. visits and 1.5 million pageviews per month (Private Interview). "Bob and George," somewhere between a pastiche of, and an homage to, the video game "Mega

26

Man," reports 1.5 million pageviews each month ("The Advertising Page") and over 500,000 unique visitors (537,859 for January 2004) ("Extreme Tracking – Bob and George).

Web Comic	Unique I.P.'s/Readers/Visitors Per Month	Pageviews/Month
Penny Arcade	3.1 Million	29 Million
Keenspot	2.5 Million	70 Million
Sinfest (Keenspot feature)	941K	5+ Million
PVP (Jan 2003)	450K	9+ Million
Sexy Losers	1 Million	6 Million
Real Life	40K, Daily	5 Million
Goats	95K	1.5 Million
Bob and George	500+K	1.5 Million

The relationship between pageviews and unique visitors / IP addresses / readers is somewhat complicated and a subject of debate. PVP's Scott Kurtz, one of the more respected businessmen in the web comics arena, provides a good "plain English" summary:

"Page impressions represent the number of times any page on the PvP site is viewed by a reader. At any one sitting, a reader could look at 10 different pages (and your ad 10 different times). So although page impressions are very accurate numbers wise, it's not quite as impressive a number once you realize that 20 impressions could equal just one potential customer.

"That's where Unique Visitors come in. This metric is a little less accurate since another name for a unique visitor is unique IP address. That means that a person who looks at the site at work, from one IP address, and then again that same day at home from another IP address would show up as two unique people. However, it works the other way as well. PvP has a lot of fans at Blizzard Entertainment and if 50 employees look at the site from the company network, that only counts as one IP address or one unique viewer" (Kurtz, "Become a PVP Sponsor"). There are two other ways to measure traffic, depending on the model of web comic site. The first is in subscribers. The site best known for its subscribers, although it has grown into a suite of sites, is Modern Tales (.com). Modern Tales, Girlamatic, Serializer.net, and Graphic Smash are anthology sites. American Elf, Jazz Age Comics, Rumble Girls, and Whimville are sites devoted to a single feature. "Around 3400 individual humans are subscribed to one or more of our sites. Around 900 of those people are subscribed to more than one site, so there are around 4300 active subscription accounts," reports Joey Manley, the owner of Modern Tales (Manley).

The last method of measuring audience is by micropayment purchasers. This method is really only 7 months old as implemented by a company called BitPass, and the mechanics of this will be discussed later in this thesis. Scott McCloud, author of *Understanding Comics*, who is also a shareholder in BitPass, has posted 2 installments of a three-part graphic novel in Flash format on his website. Each installment is available for purchase for a quarter. The first installment, over a period of 7 months, has sold 2310 copies. After an initial surge, sales have settled down to a steady 6 copies sold each day, according to McCloud. The second issue, out for 32 days, has sold 797 copies.

The business of web comics – and as you can see by the audience at the higher end of the spectrum, it is a business – is really just a microcosm of the business of online content. When looking at online content in general, and web comics specifically, certain media economics and marketing concepts come to the surface.

Metcalfe's Law of Connectivity has value when explaining the Internet. Entertainment industry economist Harold Vogel explains it as: "Assuming that a network has sufficient capacity to remain unclogged even while carrying lots of traffic, its utility (or value) rises by at least the number of users (or nodes) squared" (Vogel 227). This law has two applications. The first as Vogel notes, is that web servers can sustain multiple connections (you could define that as users or nodes, depending on your perspective) at the same time, causing the value of the Internet to increase exponentially as new nodes are added (Vogel 227-8). The second application of this law is to content. The more content that is on a site, the more there is for a viewer to look at, the more there is for a viewer to use as an entry point from a search engine, and a similar snowball effect of increasing traffic occurs.

Note the traffic statistics of Keenspot. Keenspot has fewer viewers than Penny Arcade, but dwarfs them in pageviews. Keenspot has a multitude of comic strips on their site, over 50 accessible from their homepage. Keenspot's owners call themselves a publisher. In the context of Metcalfe's Law, they are a Network unto themselves. Keenspot promotes their internal network with a "newsbox" advertising other comics on their site. "On a good day, the newsbox can generate an extra 250,000 pageviews for a small comic," Bleuel says of the initiative. "I know a lot of comics say their readership doubles or even triples immediately upon joining Keenspot" (Bleuel).

Similarly, Modern Tales reported 900 of their 3400 subscribers had multiple accounts. Not growth as drastic as Metcalfe's Law would indicate, but an illustration of the principle in action. For single feature sites, compare *Goats* and *Bob and George*. Each feature reports 1.5 million page views. *Goats* does it off 95,000 unique viewers, *Bob and George* needs over 500,000. *Goats* is a seven-year-old strip and has more nodes in the form of comics or content to look at.

The fact that having a plethora of old content, usually in the form of last year's comic strips, equates to an increased traffic illustrates that the concept of "evergreen" properties exists in a much broader capacity. The difference between an evergreen web page and something like a Disney cartoon, most of which are considered evergreen properties, is that web browsing is the equivalent of media rental, pricing to discourage ownership does not seem to apply to the web as it does to film (Vogel 94). Similarly, McCloud's steady sales of the first issue of *The Right Number* seven months after the fact indicate a longer life span than the average monthly print comic book, where conventional retail wisdom dictates interest will all but disappear the week after the comic appears on the shelf.

* Business Takeaway – Content has a longer shelf life online than in the print world. Unlike yesterday's newspaper, online content is always handy. Old topics may suddenly become of interest, and people may suddenly flock to a two-year-old article if it becomes relevant to current affairs. Similarly, the more content you have, the more people will be able to explore, should something pique interest. Keep your archives open and let search engines index them. This

applies to product descriptions, as well as creative content.

It should also be noted that web comics have grown into a wider variety of genres and formats than the printed comic book. Print comic books are largely super heroes with a smattering of science fiction, with the Archie line, almost absent from the direct market, being the main source of humor. Web comics cover a wider range of genres and super heroes is generally not one done to excess. One very popular genre is video games. *Penny Arcade* is largely a humor strip about video games. *Bob and George* is based on the Mega Man video game, specifically. *PVP* started out a video game themed strip and has evolved into a bit more of a humorous character study, but still makes the odd excursion into video game material.

Web Comics theorist and academic Scott McCloud calls this proliferation of alternate themes "side-door diversification." McCloud defines the front door as the comic book store where a reader walks in and looks at what comics are on the rack because he's already interested in comics. Citing "the gaming strip" as the first example of this, McCloud summaries the side-door theory by saying "you're reading a comic because it's something you're interested in, not because it's a comic." The side-door opportunities then expand the circle of readers (Private Interview). Other side-door examples would include *User Friendly* for the computer science crowd and *Diesel Sweeties* which maintains an unusually high demographic among women.

MIT Comparative Media Professor Henry Jenkins comments on this phenomenon in *Technology Review*, saying "many new artists are releasing their first comics online, self-publishing in order to maintain creative control. Some will be pulled into the mainstream later, they haven't forsaken any chance of drawing Batman down the line, but right now, in what has been perhaps the greatest flourishing of young talent in comics since the underground comic movement of the 1960s, they are enjoying on the fringes. These artists are targeting comics at everyone from ravers and skateboarders to sports fans, gamers and chess fanatics. They are mixing and matching comics with flash animation as well as playing with the graphic possibilities of a vastly expanded canvas. They nostalgically evoke older traditions as well as produce work that doesn't look like anything we've seen before. They offer everything from cute kids to barbed social commentary and gross bathroom humor" (Jenkins, "Will the Web Save Comics?").

* Business Takeaway – The web is a great aggregator of niche interests. Adding a different flavor to a topic, much like applying the topic of video games to the format of comic strips, can consolidate a geographically disparate, but targeted audience in one place that can't always be assembled in the real world. The web is also less expensive than creating and distributing a test issue of a niche market magazine when looking to determine a potential audience.

Chapter 4: Print Comic Book Publishers Online

One would hope that the Internet might be able to help with the problems of distribution and exposure. Distribution is a common problem for many industries and a lack of retail outlets, both in the abandonment of the newsstand and the contraction of the direct market, might liken the scenario to the music industry, when Columbia House initially established itself as a solution to distribution problems. Unlike the early days of the music industry, which enjoyed radio play, exposure may be a problem with comics. If the distribution chain has been shortened, it is unclear how a potential reader will discover comics without stumbling into a specialty retailer. The Internet could potentially serve this function for comics. Unlike the original Columbia House scenario, the existing retailers pose a potential barrier to this scenario.

Tony Panaccio offers insight into why the comic book retailers opposed many online offerings: "In 1992, there were 10,000 comic shops. This was a mix of enthusiasts and hobbyists who simply had large collections and a desire to buy new stuff at wholesale, and some business people from outside of comics who saw the speculator market as a quick way to make money.

"In the boom and bust of the speculator market in the mid-90s, those businessmen took it on the chin, leaving the enthusiasts to tough it out. With the exception of some smart comics business people like Jim Hanley and Chuck Rozanski, the majority of the surviving shops were run by enthusiasts and hobbyists, and not traditional business people. They own their shops out of their love of comics, and not because it affords them a wonderful living. But it does afford them the ability to buy their new stuff at wholesale, go to conventions and write it off on their taxes, and participate in a business as more of a VIP hobbyist. As a result, many comics retailers are not classically trained business owners.

"In just about any other industry, these retailers would have gone belly-up, but their passion for comics makes them work harder to hang on. Many didn't make it through the 90s. The ones who remain were not necessarily the smartest (as it could be argued that the smart comics retailer left the business in the 90s), but rather, the most passionate.

"Anything that threatens their core business can make them very irrational and emotional. At one point, we considered allowing comics retailers to sell subscriptions to COW [Comics On the Web, Crossgen's web comic offering] directly to their retail customers, and keep 50 percent of the subscription fees. A survey of 40 retailers on that idea sent us back to the drawing board, because many retailers could not see the upside in selling an online version of what they sold on their stands, even though COW represented an entry point for new customers for the line" (Private Interview).

When asked how a direct market comics retailer would react to comics being available for purchase online, Panaccio replies "Like a kick in the chops," and continues. "When we established our deal with Midtown Comics to be CG's official online retailer, we received nastygrams from other retailers who complained that Midtown discounted their comics too much and that we were undercutting their prices by selling direct" (Private Interview).

While Marvel does have a link to Midtown, it is not a formal arrangement, as is the case with Crossgen. On

Marvel's site, Midtown's link sits on a page with links to 5 different websites that sell comic books. It should be noted neither Crossgen nor Marvel makes it possible to buy from a page directly describing product.

Bill Jemas states that it is Marvel's policy not to sell online. "We'd rather have someone go into the comic store and buy," Jemas says, citing an obligation to the stores to sell what they've ordered (Private Interview).

That is not to say that he has not heard complaints from retailers. "We get complaints, but we don't pay attention to complaints," Jemas explains. Jemas finds that the top 500 retailers make up the majority of Marvel's sales and that the "smarter retailers love the Internet promotions." (Private Interview)

While Panaccio and Jemas represent different perspectives in print comic book publishing and have different rationales for their policies, both agree that retailers have adverse reactions to online sales and promotions and that the presence of the retailers has influenced their thinking on online sales, despite the Internet's ability to reach into geographies where direct market retail outlets do not exist. (And, in illustration to this convergence of their normally inverse stances, Panaccio refers to independent publishers as VIP hobbyists, while Jemas more diplomatically refers to a minority of "smarter retailers.") Forrester Research VP calls this kind of channel conflict the "thorniest issue of all on the Internet," and warns that traditional sales channel partners can be detrimental when it comes to the Internet, blocking sales growth and causing potential customers to become frustrated and cease trying to buy an item or brand when they cannot easily purchase a product from a company site that has been reduced to strictly marketing content by aggressive channel partners

(Modahl pp. 169-171). This state of sales channel conflict is all too real in the realm of print comic books, and sets the picture for an examination of the online presences of print comic book publishers.

However, before we get into the Internet adoption of the print companies, it is appropriate to mention their order cycle. The direct market is based on non-returnable orders, so publishers are able to make printing more of an economic efficiency, if they so choose. Marvel, the largest publisher, prints only to fulfill initial orders. This system can cause problems if the retailers significantly under-estimate demand for a comic, especially in the case of Marvel, which prints only to fill initials orders and very seldom reprints individual issues prior to book-format collection. The solicitation cycle has traditionally begun 3 months prior to the shipping month of a comic, with orders being due 2 months prior. Marvel has recently moved this up to approximately 20 days prior to an individual book's shipping, and it is unclear if other publishers will follow, but the ordering process is significantly ahead of consumer purchase with a non-returnable product.

In 2002, Marvel Comics was, by far, the most successful print comic book publisher, in terms of the readership of their web-based comics, or "dotComics," as the company has branded the Flash-driven format. "The technique is a translation of a printed comic into a slightly animated Flash format. Comic pages appear on the screen, a few panels at a time, with word balloons bloating over the characters. Larger panels sometimes scroll from side-to-side in cinematic fashion, but it's essentially, despite the tweaks, the same comic book found in a store" (Allen, "Dot-Comics Lure New Readers").

With the May 2002 release of the film version of Spider-Man, downloads of the dotComics soared to 3.27 million copies. These digital copies were frequently put online when a print comic had sold out at the retail level, so that readers would not miss the first chapter of a story, as well as for general promotion reasons. In at least one instance, a dotComic was found to have been downloaded in greater numbers than were sold in print (Allen, "Dot-Comics Lure New Readers").

The dotComic program was partially discontinued in early 2003. While several are still available for download and viewing on Marvel's website, new ones are not currently being produced. Jemas gives two reasons. First, retailers have adjusted to Marvel's no reprint policy and have started ordering in sufficient numbers to avoid quick sell-outs, so Marvel has been more inclined to issue "Marvel Must Have" print editions – slightly discounted volumes of recently sold out comics – instead of just putting new dotComics online. Second, it was felt that the first few issues of "Ultimate Spider-Man" were the best introduction for a new reader, so those were left up, instead of using issues later in the series. Jemas estimates that the use of dotComics as both previews and supplements for sold out issues caused an approximate 5% uptick in sales (Private Interview).

* Business Takeaway – If your primary product is content, there are no inventory concerns online. Unlike a book or a magazine, your product is replicated when a person types in your URL or clicks a link. The same applies to eBooks. When an eBook is purchased, the download is an instant replication. If your product is supported by advertising or subscription, this makes the web an ideal medium for mass distribution.

Crossgen operates a website named "Comics on the Web" (.com) which features slightly animated digital editions of their print comics. Tony Panaccio puts the number of subscribers at 5000 when he left Crossgen. Since then, Crossgen's digital editions have started appearing on AOL and AOL has driven "4 million hits in the last month" to the Comics on the Web. (Private Interview.) It is difficult to say exactly how many of those hits have been converted to subscriptions. Vin Crosbie writes that the average adoption rate of users subscribing to an online paper or magazine that was previously free of charge is 1% (Crosbie). Were that to hold true, that would mean an additional 40,000 subscribers. If the adoption rate were half that, an addition 20,000 subscribers would be added. Crossgen's highest selling title is normally around or just above 20,000 and it is entirely possible their web subscribers may outnumber their print buyers. It is a situation well worth monitoring. Still, at $2 per subscriber per month, Comics On the Web brings in $10,000 each month and has enjoyed some promotional success.

"With Way of the Rat #1, we released the book for free on Comics On the Web two weeks before it hit the stands," Panaccio reports. "It sold 24 percent more copies than the previous #1 launch, Ruse. We did the same thing with The Path #1, and reorders were heavy, more than 1,000 per week, for about four weeks. Preorders close about 45 days before the issue is shipped, so all of the increase in both cases came in the form of reorders." (Private Interview).

* Business Takeaway – Giving away samples online works. Exposing a product in a risk-free medium will build a following in brick and mortar world. The more limited your distribution, the greater your potential

reward. Notice that Marvel, the industry leader, would sustain 5% growth using established properties, while Crossgen, a relative newcomer, could affect 20%+ growth by fostering familiarity with completely new products.

As was mentioned previously Crossgen did maintain a relationship with Midtown Comics (.com) to sell their comics to consumers via the web. While the link to the Midtown website is located in the shopping section, away from product descriptions, and the generic Crossgen product page at Midtown's website takes three clicks to get to, Panaccio says they occasionally did upwards of $10,000 per month off that link, which was more profitable for Crossgen, since Midtown bought product directly from them, while accounting for under 5% of Crossgen's overall business (Private Interview).

By 2004, the most common use of the web by print publishers is to have listings of upcoming comics. Some publishers have extensive previews with actual pages. DC alternates between highlighted excerpts of finished pages from highlighted projects and unlettered, black and white pages from others. Marvel, on the other hand, offers only listings. Formats vary from an inline graphic to a .PDF file. Some publishers, like Image and Oni, will have complete copies of certain out of print comics books online, to promote interest in a series. Others, like DC and Dark Horse, do not.

Three companies of any size offer links to purchase directly from product descriptions: Dark Horse, Oni, and Avatar. Image and DC don't even have a retailer linked off their website.

The print publishers are most likely further hampered by the lack of a trusted brand name from which web-based customers could order their products. Many book publishers opt to refer customers to Amazon, in lieu of selling directly. There is no universally trusted vendor like Amazon for the comic book space, nor is there an affiliate program as readily implemented as Amazon's. Yet, this is the confused state of print comic book publishers venturing into the online space.

Ultimately, channel conflict has splintered the print publishers. There is a fear in many places to sell directly online. There is even a reluctance to fully utilize the medium for preview purposes, even though it has been demonstrated to be effective. The direct market sales channel becomes a gilded caged. The publishers lament a lack of additional outlets, but either out of fear or a sense of obligation, ultimately bow to demand of the retail channel, so that if the channel were to contract further, any problems resulting from further loss of outlets would become, in a sense, a self-fulfilling prophecy. Of the publishers with direct links to purchase their products, only Dark Horse is a premiere publisher with Diamond: it is the smallest of the group. Oni and Avatar are firmly in the category of small press. Perhaps they feel they are already suffering the consequences of the system and no further punishment from the retail channel will occur. And Crossgen, while only indirectly linking to an online purchasing channel, is the only publisher to sell their content as a web feature. Even without the influx of AOL traffic it ranks as the largest subscription base for a web comic.

* Business Takeaway – Be aware of how your distribution channels will react to online competition. Some will have no problem, some may interpret it as

unfair competition. Sometimes a compromise can be reached involving the parameters of how you sell your own product online. Depending on your distribution, you might be better off offending a percentage of your retail outlets or it might cost you more business than you pick-up online. This is something that should only be evaluated on a case by case basis.

Chapter 4A: Recent History of Print Publishers Online

CrossGen's Bankruptcy

Shortly after the original study ended, Crossgen comics filed for bankruptcy. As time would reveal, the company was carrying a great deal of debt and when additional financing failed to materialize, Crossgen shut down very quickly. Its assets were bought by Disney in auction.

From a web comics perspective, this is tragedy, in that while Crossgen had come to an arrangement to distribute digital copies of its titles on AOL, time ran out on the company before they had opportunity to monetize those online copies. Plans were being made to expand the commerce options at both the AOL and Comics on the Web. Plans were also being made to introduce advertising into the online comics. It did not come to pass.

Marvel's dotComics

Marvel has changed their policies towards online comics and previews multiple times. Since mid-2005, they have settled into a pattern of uploading the first issue of a new collected edition. This puts the experience clearly in the category of a marketing tool, with a pitch to buy the comic and a comic store locator on the interstitial page before the comic loads.

The Independent Publishers Step Up

It's now common for most independent publishers to at least give a few pages of preview material for a new book. Increasingly, there will be an archive of first issues to introduce readers to a title. Image does this in a navigation window that loads one an image of one page at

a time. Oni offers downloads in the .CBR format favored
by torrent downloaders.

DC Sticks a Toe in the Water

In December of 2006, a far cry from the online initiative
Business 2.0 was expecting, DC decided to use vintage
tactic started by Marvel in 2001 and since used by others
like Image – they make 1st issues of various series from
their Vertigo imprint available online, although they do it
in a very quick and dirty fashion. The format is a
download of a .PDF file. No Digital Rights Management
issues, but it can also be a slow download. The *Saga of
the Swamp Thing* preview registers as a 38.7MB file! DC
also eschews placing a marketing pitch in the file. Still,
with DC, baby steps are steps in the right direction.

For a look at DC doing something more interesting with
web comics, flip ahead to Chapter 5A and read about their
acquisition of the print rights for *MegaTokyo*.

Also see Chapter 6A for print publishers experimenting
with the popular new paid download model.

Chapter 5: Web Comics in Print

Just as the print publishers have experimented with putting their comics online, web cartoonists have sought to put their comics in print. There are two schools of thought that pervade these hard copy pursuits. The first school of thought is the traditionalist. The web cartoonist initially encountered his strip in a comic book, or perhaps in a newspaper and wishes to gain a sense of added legitimacy by having a print copy that can be held. The second school of thought is more capitalistic. There is a demand for these web comics in a portable collection, and it's easier to charge for a printed book than it is for access to a website.

Not every web comic has a printed edition, but many do. Scott McCloud, for instance, shuns print editions as he tries to push the boundaries of web comics in ways that print cannot duplicate, such as his "Right Number" web comic where the panel collapses inside itself revealing a new panel each time you click. Such things are not ideally suited for print reproduction. Realistically, print editions of web comics should be looked at as a form of merchandising for that reason. It's not the initial product, per se, and it will not work as well for every feature.

There are 3 sales channels for the print editions of web comics: online, direct market, and bookstores. All markets are not universally open to web comics looking for a print spin-off, but all markets have, at least, been tested by a web comic.

Online sales are the primary venue. It is a relatively simple matter to sell a paperback edition of a web strip off that strip's web site and, in many cases, Amazon. "Goats" has seven year's worth of material to reprint and recently released their third reprint volume. *Goats* cartoonist Jon Rosenberg says the sales of the reprint editions snowball as both the popularity of the strip continues to grow and new volumes are released. Sales for the paperback editions are approaching 1000 and his expectations for new volumes are closer to 2000, factoring in growth. Rosenberg also issues a limited hardcover edition of his works, targeted at the more devoted members of his audience, noting that he had 250 "premium" subscribers paying $20 per year for exclusive site features and were disposed towards larger purchases. (Private Interview)

Chris Crosby, co-owner of the web comics publisher/portal "Keenspot" reports similar online sales numbers. "Online we sold 1,500 copies of the $19.95 EXPLOITATION NOW: SELLING OUT FOR FUN & PROFIT collection and 500 of the $29.95 hardcover edition, and we generally sell at least 1,000 copies online of any other book we do," Crosby specifies. (Crosby)

David Allen, owner of Plan 9 Publishing, a company that prints book collections of web comics, reports that his average print run for a web comic collection is 500, and that he bases his print runs on a six month supply, so his average annual sales on a book would be approximately 1000 copies. His highest print run was a recent batch of 3000 copies (estimating a demand for 6000 sales in 12 months). Given multiple printing, Allen says he has several books that have sold over 10,000 copies over the years. Much as was opined by Rosenberg, and also by McCloud on the topic of his micropayment comics, Allen says that there will be a steady, if smaller, stream of sales on a title after an initial surge, and with each new book in a series, demand will increase for the previous installments. Allen also notes, anecdotally, that titles in his catalog have a tendency to cross-sell. This would seem to indicate that the laws of networking and evergreen media function with the online sales of web comic print collections, as well as with the web comics themselves (Private Interview).

Allen says at least 90 % of his business comes from online transactions and the bulk of that comes from the artists' websites, where the strips are shown. Less than 10% of the business comes through retail channels, including Amazon (Private Interview).

The bookstore market is an unusual one for web comics to crack. There have been four well-known excursions into the bookstore by web comics. *User Friendly* has a number of titles issued by O'Reilly, best known for their "In a Nutshell" series of technical manuals. Sales figures for that are not available. The Matrix, the popular film franchise of recent years, issued a print collection of the online comic books they'd used as promotional pieces. The Bookscan "adult graphic novels" report, which claims to cover roughly 75% of bookstore markets, in its week of 12/31/03 report, indicates that the print collection of the Matrix had sold 8171 copies, year-to-date. Especially impressive for a book with a November release date. *Megatokyo*, a web comic popular for the rights to its next reprint volume to be picked up by Dark Horse, was listed as selling 11,576 copies of their first book in 2003 (Bookscan). The actual sales numbers for bookstores will be larger, although exactly how much larger is difficult to say, as the 25% of outlets not reporting may not stock comic material, print or web, in great numbers.

Finally, though it is too soon to have sales figures, Keenspot has recently entered into the bookstore space. Crosby reports the need to go back to press after fulfilling bookstore demand for 3000 copies. Unfortunately, the timing of the retail re-orders is too soon to ascertain what the exact sales levels of the initial 3000 books in the system are. Meanwhile, a second book is scheduled for release shortly (Crosby).

While that does sound positive for Keenspot, it should be noted that print comic publisher Fantagraphics very nearly went bankrupt, largely due to overprinting their books after initial bookstore success (Richman). Plan 9 Publishing, which does not issue returnable books, echoes this concern and notes that the pay cycle for an author can easily stretch out to a year, depending on when bookstore returns are issued and questions if returned copies will really be in salable condition. (Private Interview)

The direct market is another market with sporadic entry by web comics. While Diamond is the predominant force in distribution to this market, with estimates between 90-97%, it is not the only player. Jon Rosenberg recently began shipping "Goats" trade paperbacks through Cold Cut Distributors and reports sending under 50 to the distributor, initially (Private Interview).

Still, the major business in this market is Diamond. Keenspot did release a few standard format comic books in the direct market, but eventually abandoned that in favor of the book format and greener pastures online and in bookstores (Crosby). Direct market retailer and columnist Brian Hibbs shows ICV2's estimates of The Matrix's print edition at 8285, and issues a warning that with the reports that Diamond issues and that ICV2 issues their estimates on, there is often no way to judge re-orders and that they do exist (Hibbs). Also in the direct market with a trade paperback is Megatokyo, whose first volume with Dark Horse is reported as selling 3,295 by

ICV2, Diamond's ninth-highest graphic novel order for January 2004. It should be noted that numbers 48 through 50 on the bestseller list for that month are all estimated at 1,247 copies, very close to average sales for a book in the web comic online channel (ICV2, "Top 50").

PVP is the rare example of a web comic in an actual comic book format. Coming out bi-monthly under the Image Comics imprint, *PVP*'s print offspring feature web strips with some added material, and it does fairly well. ICV2 estimates issue 5, from December 2003 at 8,253 copies, some 2,000 copies above top-selling independent black and white comics like *Cerebus* and *Queen & Country* (ICV2, "Top 300).

It is interesting to note, while the penetration of product is not as great in the bookstore and direct market channels, the few instances of appearance seem to be performing relatively well. Matrix, in fairness, takes on a life of its own and is probably best discarded as a statistical anomaly. It is also interesting that the direct market retailers do not "cry foul" over the content being online, as they have with Marvel and Crossgen, nor does this seem to have hurt anyone's sales – particularly *Megatokyo* in the bookstores, where it has outsold much of DC and Marvel's trade paperbacks.

Seth Godin, the Internet marketing expert and author, likes to talk about using the web to distribute free content and create an "Idea Virus" around a product, which is a jargonistic way of saying using the content to creative word of mouth advertising around product, pre-launch. He went so far as to offer free .PDF format downloads of his book, *The Idea Virus*, prior to publication and listed it in his book as example of that type of promotion (Godin, pp. 124-5). His book went on to do quite well and his theory is applicable to the print efforts of web comics. The material is presented in a free digital edition and, as Godin puts it, enough people read part of it and like it sufficiently to buy the hard copy. With the web comics, there is an additional value added in the content being all in one package in the book, as opposed to scattered with one or two strips on each page online. David Allen agrees on this point, emphasizing the individual websites as the source of his sales (Private Interview).

* Business Takeaway – Popularity online does translate into popularity in the physical world. While the primary market is still ordering from the originating website, online properties are slowing making their way into bookstores and in some instances, producing similar sales to traditional print products.

Chapter 5A: Collected Editions Get Super-Sized

Once, an emerging option for web comics, printed collected editions are now a staple of the business model, and generating enough heat for the traditional print publisher to jump in. Tracking the sales of these web comic print editions can be problematic, as the vast majority of them are sold directly off the individual comic's website and aren't sold in Bookscan-surveyed venues or sold through Diamond. To examine their increased popularity, there are three tools available: self-reporting, Bookscan reports, and Diamond distribution estimates.

Caveats: Bookscan represents actual sales at retail outlets, but is only around 70% of the retail market. Information gathered in the this study is gathered from the last Bookscan report for the graphic novels category and will not yield data for graphic novels not making the top 750 in sales for the final week of the year. Similarly, Diamond estimates are typically regarded as 20% below actual direct market sales, and reorders of under 1000 copies per month will typically not be visible on sales charts. ICV2(.com) estimates are used here.

The first web comic to make a big splash in traditional publishing circles was MegaTokyo. Now on its third publisher, and the subject of bidding wars, from I.C.E. to major independent publisher Dark Horse Comics, and now "Big Two" publisher, DC Comics, is vicariously participating in the web comics scene by publishing MegaTokyo through their "CMX Manga" imprint.

MegaTokyo's estimated sales are as follows:

2003 (Titles released by I.C.E.)
MEGATOKYO CHAPTER ONE 1,744 (Diamond Only)
MEGATOKYO CHAPTER ZERO: RELAX   11,576
(Bookscan Only)

2004 (Titles released by Dark Horse)
MEGATOKYO V1 -   12,899 (Bookscan)   80%
               3,233 (Diamond)   20%
               16,132 (Total)

MEGATOKYO V2 -   19,415 (Bookscan)   82.5%
               4,102 (Diamond)   17.5%
               23,517 (Total)

2005 (Titles released by Dark Horse)
MEGATOKYO V1   8,612 (Bookscan)
MEGATOKYO V2   7,580 (Bookscan)
MEGATOKYO V3   19,554 (Bookscan) 82%
               4,191 (Diamond)   18%
               23,745 (Total)

2006 (Title released by DC)
MEGATOKYO V4 -   16,331 (Bookscan) 79%
               4,385(Diamond) 21%
               20,716 (Total)

We find the reported sales over the three year period where MegaTokyo was published by Dark Horse to be an extremely consistent 80%-82.5% Bookscan/retail sales to 17.5% - 20% Diamond/direct market sales ratio for new releases. It is reasonable to assume some backlist sales did occur in the direct market in 2005 and 2006, but was under the reporting threshold. It is also reasonable to assume the percentage of Bookscan/retail is a little lower in 2006, given V4 was released mid-year, instead of January or February, as previous volumes had been.

Penny Arcade entered the print arena in 2006, but their sales levels are something of an enigma, with the available data points almost contradictory.

PENNY ARCADE VOL 1 ATTACK O/T BACON ROBOTS TP –
    3,914 (Diamond)

PENNY ARCADE VOL 2 LEGENDS MAGIC SWORD TP –
    7,280 (Bookscan) 65%
    3,897 (Diamond) 35%
    11,177 (Total)

It is safe to assume that the first volume just didn't chart in the last week in December on Bookscan and ran a similar number to the second volume. However, we need to factor in two other pieces of information: an ICV2 report that the first volume of Penny Arcade quickly sold out of a 30,000 copy print run, and Penny Arcade's Business Manager, Robert Khoo, believes that of their print sales "less than 10% come from comic books stores." Given the initial sell-out, a second printing and a total of 40-50K copies sold would not sound unreasonable and fit Khoo's estimate. It would also likely mean Penny Arcade sells an enormous amount of books off their own website.

Also going through Diamond, but not appearing on Bookscan is Scott Kurtz's extremely popular PVP strip.

2004
PVP VOL 1 DORK AGES TP –   2,259 (Diamond Only)
PVP ARCHIVES VOL 1 AT LARGE TP – 1,012 (Diamond Only)

2005
PVP RELOADED VOL 2 TP –   1,393 (Diamond Only)

Volumes 3 and 4 did not chart with Diamond. It is extremely likely, much as with Penny Arcade, that PVP does a much better business directly through its own site.

Phil Foglio's Girl Genius, notable for having ceased printing monthly comics, in favor of web comics, had 2 volumes chart at Diamond in 2006

GIRL GENIUS VOL 4 TP - 1,480
GIRL GENIUS VOL 5 TP - 2,054

"Traditional" magazine formatted comic books, relative to the market, do not fare as well at Diamond, with PVP steadily dropping in initial sales and Athena Voltaire, a blip on the radar.

2003
PVP Series 5 issues- 46,185 Total; Average 9,237/issue
2004
PVP Comic - 7 issues - 50,326 total; 7,190/issue average
2005
PVP Comic - 8 issues, 50,302(total); 6,288/issue average
2006
PVP Comic - 7 issues - 36,777 total; 5,254 average/issue
Athena Voltaire: Flight of the Falcon #1 (Speakeasy
                                    Edition): 2,718
                                    (Ape Edition): 2,054

All this is not to say appearing on the Bookscan and Diamond charts is the real measure of success. Howard Tayler has sold 5,000 copies of his Schlock Mercenary web comics (split roughly 3,000 – 2,000 between two volumes) directly off his site. ICV2 reports Jorge Cham has sold 12,000 and 7,000 copies, respectively, of two volumes of his "Piled Higher and Deeper" web comics, as of April 2006. Cham sells it directly through his site and through the Baker & Taylor book distributor to bookstores.

The available data suggests that the direct market for comic books is either under-served or unreceptive of web comics. Whether this reflects a lack of awareness from retailers for ordering in or a lack of purchase interest from consumers is unclear, although of the 4 web comics that have cracked Diamond's top 100 list for graphic novels, all but PVP have exhibited growth in initial orders, so lack of awareness may be more of a factor in this case.

Certainly, it is most profitable for a web comic to sell printed editions off its own website. This can save anywhere from 40-60% in distributor discounts and can mean the difference between a profit and a loss on short runs. A benefit of the direct market is the absence of returns. The possibility of returned books should be strongly considered before entering into traditional bookstore distribution, especially for smaller strips. A palatable alternative to mass returns is entering into a direct relationship with Amazon. Amazon is conservative in its stocking habits, saving you large scale returns in almost all cases, and will require a 55% discount for their "Amazon Advantage" program.

Another option used by a number of smaller web comics is Print On Demand. This comes in two flavors, the first being commercial services like Lightning Source and BookSurge which require ISBN numbers and set-up fees, but also place you in the bookstore distribution system (frequently on a non-returnable basis, which means bookstores _can_ order you, but almost certainly will only do so for customer requests, however such arrangements do get you universally listed in online bookstores, such as Amazon and Bn.com).

The second option, and the more popular at this point, is services like Lulu.com and Comixpress.com. These POD services, on a per unit basis, are quite expensive, relative to traditional printing or use of a commercial POD service. You will not be able to sell through a distributor or Amazon with one of these services and break even without having a ridiculous cover price. On the other hand, there is no set-up fee for Lulu, a negligible one for Comixpress and no ISBN number required for either, so they're easy for cartoonists with no budget and/or a small audience. These services are essentially direct-to-consumer tools. The consumer is directed to the Lulu or Comixpress site, where they make the purchase and a commission is sent to the cartoonist. The commission will depend on page count and retail pricing, but is generally $1-3. With a commercially printed book sold directly, especially if the interior is in black and white, the margin would be more in the $5 - $10 range.

POD is a useful tool, particularly for black & white interior art, and when used with a commercial service, but it can also be tailored for smaller publications.

* Business Takeaway – Printed editions are now a completely accepted merchandising extension of a web comic and there are a variety of methods available that allow for scaling to fit an individual property's circumstance. There is no reason not to at least experiment with a print edition.

*Business Takeaway – Always start selling a printed edition off your own website. While some consumers may prefer Amazon, you can keep at least an extra 40% of the product's price. Expand as opportunity permits, but this is a business that starts at home and home is your homepage in this case. Remember, your audience knows you from your website and that's the first place they'll look for the book.

*Business Takeaway – Don't ignore the direct market. If your printing arrangement allows you enough margin for the required discount, there may be an audience in comic shops. While it isn't as easily done, you also aren't required to use Diamond. It is possible, if time consuming, to solicit comic shops directly or use a niche distributor like Cold Cut.

Chapter 5B: Web Comics Break Into Newsprint

2004 saw more web comics break into the newspaper market... by giving their content away. PVP appeared in the Kansas City Star and Philadelphia Evening Bulletin. Keenspot packaged a full comics page which appears in the Turlock (California) Journal. Both PVP and Keenspot offered the strips to newspapers for free, seeking to use the newspaper appearances as ads for their website, thus increasing traffic and the audience base for merchandising. Keenspot additionally has built space into their comics page that could be sold as advertising, building in a potential direct revenue stream into the product.

This gave way to setbacks, as PVP didn't last and the pioneering cross-over strip, "Helen, Sweetheart of the Internet" has gone into "sabbatical" and is presumed discontinued.

And then in January of 2007, Diesel Sweeties made the jump to syndication with United Media. It should be noted that United Media has recruited existing web comics for inclusion on their Comics.com website in the past, and that their new talent scout, Ted Rall, has some history with a number of web-based cartoonists.

Below the radar, Piled Higher and Deeper is syndicated in 9 college newspapers, at institutions like Stanford, MIT and Georgia Tech.

These intrusions into the world of newspapers have alarmed some syndicated cartoonists who see this as a threat to their livelihood. It brings up some interesting points. Strips like Peanuts, Garfield and Dilbert have made their fortunes off licensing – reprint books, stuffed animal, clothing and the like. From the view of a web cartoonist like Kurtz, syndication money is a secondary concern towards licensing and merchandising. Syndication is just a publicity vehicle. Were newspapers to agree with this principle, it could derail comic strip syndication. While this is a huge philosophical leap, and the adoption of the free strips is by no means widespread, this is a situation that merits watching.

Chapter 6: Revenue Models

The revenue model for the direct market is very straightforward. Over 90% of the market is controlled by Diamond Comics Distributors. Diamond requires a 60-70% discount to carry a comic book (Diamond, "The Product Life Cycle"). Tony Panaccio informs that the standard discount is 61% (Private Interview). Diamond further stipulates, should it accept your comic for distribution, the product should sell at least $2,500 retail within 3-5 issues or they will most likely discontinue selling it (Diamond, "Diamond's Terms & Conditions of Sale.").

The standard price for a comic book is $2.95. Some of DC and Marvel's more popular titles retail for $2.25, $2.50 or $2.75. A small number of low print run independents are starting to use a $3.50 cover price. By and large, unless the comic is from DC or Marvel, the cover price will be $2.95.

Right off the bat, this tells us two things:

1)   848 copies of a $2.95 priced comic book will keep you in Diamond's good graces (715 of a $3.50-priced comic book). That's a rather small amount and it will shortly be proven that anyone failing to meet that sales level will almost certainly be losing money on the venture.

2)   At a 61% discount, a publisher will receive $1.15 every time Diamond sells $2.95-priced book ($1.365 for a $3.50-priced book).

The direct market is simple, elegant, and economically efficient. Barring an extremely late shipping date, there are no returns of product. Diamond takes the orders. The publisher prints the book and ships it to Diamond. Diamond pays net 30 (within 30 days of receipt of product). The publisher will know whether or not the books will break even before the order to print is made. The only variable is whether or not the publisher wishes to print extra copies for potential re-orders.

There are two perspectives from which to evaluate the revenues from a print comic: publisher and cartoonist. Publisher is rather straightforward: revenue minus materials. Cartoonists can evaluate it three different ways. Should the cartoonist be a self-publisher, the formula is still appropriate. Scott McCloud, a former champion of creator's rights when the self-publishing scene was in its heyday in the 1980s, objects to this as an effective measure, citing the small number of self-published comics currently still in existence. He feels a more appropriate measure would be a 10% royalty off retail (Private Interview). As 10% might not include the total creative budget (writer, artist, letterer and occasionally colorist), 20% royalty will also be assessed here for comparative purposes. Finally, as more appropriate when dealing with DC and Marvel, there is the simple measure of creative budget. Bill Jemas lists Marvel's standard creative budget for a comic book at $14,000, although the split between creators will vary (Private Interview).

A printing quote was obtained from Morgan Printing, a firm that prints comic books like *Teenage Mutant Ninja Turtles*, and *Supernatural Law*, for the color and black white comic books with the following specifications:

"Description- 32g plus cover saddle stitched book Copy-output entire book electronically from information furnished by customer.

Size- 6 5/8 x 10 1/4
Stock- text- 40lb offset
Cover- 80lb enamel text
Colors of ink- text- 4-color process throughout vs. black
only text cover- four color process covers outside cover
only, black inside covers"

Color

Quantity	1,000	5,000	8,000	10,000
Price	$2,375.00	$3,395.00	$4,295.00	$4,895.00
Price/copy	$2.375	$0.679	$0.536875	$0.4895

Black and White

Quantity	1,000	3,000	5,000	7,000
Price	$1,270.00	$1,580.00	$1,913.00	$2,253.00
Price/copy	$1.27	$0.5267	$0.3826	$0.3219

In addition to the cost of printing, there is also a shipping
charge to move the comic books to the distributor's
warehouse. Morgan Printing indicated that 2000 comic
books would weigh very close to 250 pounds and that UPS
was often used to ship the books. Quotes were run on the
UPS web site to ship 1,000, 5,000 and 10,000 books with
each shipment insured at cover value of the comic books
contained. The shipping cost per book started out at
slightly over 7 cents per book ($0.0783) and rose to
slightly over 9 cents per book ($.0.09379) when shipping
10,000 (UPS).

Being conservative and adding 9 cents to the cost of a
comic book (7 cents for a 1000 print run) and rounding to
the nearest cent changes the cost tables to:

Color

Quantity	1,000	5,000	8,000	10,000
Price/copy	$2.45	$0.77	$0.63	$0.58

Black and White

Quantity	1,000	3,000	5,000	7,000
Price/copy	$1.34	$0.62	$0.47	$0.41

Going back to the incoming revenue from Diamond, a comic book with a $2.95 cover price, regardless of color cannot make money selling 1,000 copies. It will not happen. At a $3.50 cover price ($1.365), should the shipping numbers hold fast and no incidental expenses turn up, a profit of 2.5 cents per issue could be attained. With 1000 copies, that would be a profit of $25. Or, to quote a favorite joke of Scott McCloud, "What's the difference between a comic book artist and a pizza? A pizza can feed a family of four" (Private Interview).

Going back and adjusting and calculating net revenues for comic books at these benchmark sales levels, from essentially Diamond's minimum order to the functional cap for an independent book [note: for color books, while Crossgen and IDW do occasionally near 20,000 in sales, they are part of established lines of publications and it is unlikely an individual newcomer would reach those levels without a great deal of marketing effort and time for word of mouth to accumulate. Bill Jemas also suggests 10,000 as an upper limit for independent sales (Private Interview).]

Color

Quantity	1,000	5,000	8,000	10,000
Price/copy	$2.45	$0.77	$0.63	$0.58
Total Revenue @ $2.95 ($1.15 net)	($1300)	$1900	$4160	$5700
Total Revenue @ $3.50 ($1.365 net)	($1085)	$2975	$5880	$7850

Black and White

Quantity	1,000	3,000	5,000	7,000
Price/copy	$1.34	$0.62	$0.47	$0.41
Total Revenue @ $2.95 ($1.15 net)	($190)	$1590	$3400	$5180
Total Revenue @ $3.50 ($1.365 net)	$25	$2235	$4475	$6685

As the above charts demonstrate, there is very little revenue available from independently publishing a comic book until the upper limits of what appears to be the sales barrier. If those numbers are split between multiple creators or between a publisher and the creative team there would appear to be very little money in the business and it is questionable if this could sustain a corporate structure.

Going by McCloud's royalty as a measure of income, the following chart allows for 10% and 20% royalty rates at intervals up to 26,000 copies, the approximate sales level of Dark Horse's top seller for December 2003 (ICV2. "Top 300.").

	1,000	3,000	5,000	8,000	10,000
$2.95 @ 10%	$295	$885	$1,475	$2,360	$2,950
$2.95 @ 20%	$590	$1,770	$2,950	$4,720	$5,900
$3.50 @ 10%	$350	$1,050	$1,750	$2,800	$3,500
$3.50 @ 20%	$700	$2,100	$3,500	$5,600	$7,000

	15,000	20,000	26,000
$2.95 @ 10%	$4,425	$5,900	$7,670
$2.95 @ 20%	$8,850	$1,180	$15,340
$3.50 @ 10%	$5,250	$7,000	$9100
$3.50 @ 20%	$10,500	$14,000	$18,200

It should be noted that the top selling, non-extra length, comic priced at $3.50 is 7,379 copies as estimated by ICV2 for December 2003, as not to raise expectations unreasonably (ICV2. "Top 300."). Comparing these flat royalty rates with net revenues reveals, unless the company has significant discounts from printing multiple books, it would take 5,000 copies of a black and white comic or 8,000 copies of a color comic before the publisher would start to be taking in more revenue than was being paid out in royalties. Once more, if we look at the 20% rate as the creative budget, (with a distributor discount of 61%, 20% of retail equates to 51% of net revenue), should the duties be split up between multiple creators, as is most often the case with print comic books, once more, there seems to be very little money involved until the upper levels of sale.

DC and Marvel offer a flat rate and then commission above a certain sales level. As stated earlier, Marvel's standard creative budget is $14,000 for an issue. DC's is assumed to be in the same range. Naturally, certain talent on certain books may warrant a higher budget.

Image Comics is a wild card in this area. Image charges a flat fee and the creators of the comic book take all revenues past cost and that fee. New Image creator and long-time journalist Mike San Giacomo revealed that flat fee to be $2500 in his weekly column documenting his attempts to publish a comic book. (San Giacomo)

Perhaps the most common content-based genre of website is the newspaper site. In the paper "Digital News: Content, Delivery, and Value Propositions for an Intangible Product" for the *Journal of End User Computing*, Palmer & Eriksen note that 100% of the U.S.-based newspapers they surveyed and 80% of the world newspaper utilized advertising, notably banner ads, in their online advertising model. Similarly 25% of U.S.-based and 20% of world newspapers surveyed utilized some form of subscription as part of the online revenue model. (Palmer & Eriksen, pp. 11-19) In keeping with this line of thinking, and as noted earlier, Vin Crosbie's research indicates that when an online newspaper or magazine switches from free viewing to a subscription or pay-per-view basis, there is an average customer retention of 1% (Crosbie) With web comics defined as a function of online content, let us look at revenue models involved.

In *Principles of Internet Marketing*, Ward Hanson defines Internet "Revenue-Based Business Models" in terms of "Provider-Based Revenue Models" like banner advertising and content sponsorship; and "User-Based Revenue Models," which includes product sales and "pay-per-use" (which would encompass both subscriptions and micropayments). Ward notes, "hybrid business models are common online" (Hanson, p. 125 - 138). When examining web comics, it is best to simplify the models to advertising, subscription, micropayment, donation, merchandising, and hybrid.

Advertising most commonly comes in the form of banner ads. Banner ads are commonly sold in CPM units, a standard advertising measure. In *Marketing Management*, Russell S. Winer defines CPM as Cost Per Thousand (M being the Roman numeral one thousand) (Winer p. 248). Thus, the value of one viewer of a Web comic supported by a single banner ad is the CPM Rate divided by 1000. Banner ads can also come in CPC (Cost Per Click) and CPA (Cost Per Action) formats which require the viewer to either click on the ad or perform an action before a larger commission is paid. CPM and CPC are often mixed.

Finding an average price for a CPM is an attempt to hit a moving target. Rates will change from site to site, with differences in demographics, and in some cases by the skill of the salesman, with large differences between banners targeted to a specific site and "run of network" ads used to fill inventory by advertising networks. Burst Media, a popular banner ad network specializing in content-based websites, reports the average CPM for a run of network 480x60 pixel banner is $0.85 cents (Private Interview). At the top end of the market, *Penny Arcade's* rate card lists their CPM for the two banners they offer at $5.00 and $5.50 ("Rate Card"). Advertising accounts for 55% of Penny Arcade's revenues (Khoo). *MegaTokyo* charges between $1.59 - $1.30 CPM for banner ads ("Support MegaToyko"). Jon Rosenberg says that *Goats* was having some minor success with a "self-serve" $1 CPM, but was going to drop advertising to increase his focus on merchandising. *Sexy Losers* charges a $1.25 CPM ("Bald Rocket") and its anonymous artist "Hard" estimates its sell-through at 10-15% of inventory (Hard). Keenspot offers a range from $1.25 - $1.00 CPM. ("Keenspot – Rate Card") Keenspot's Darren Bleuel says they sell about 5% of their inventory, do offer bulk discounts, and get around a $0.15 CPM through the third-party networks they use to fill out the inventory (Bleuel). The network CPM for Keenspot is disturbingly low and probably indicative of the need to fill up some 70 million pages with advertising. Some other strips report sub-$1.00 CPMs, but nothing as low as $0.15. What emerges is a range from $5.50 to $0.15CPM, with $1.00 - $1.25 being the most common rate for a targeted site. It is additionally likely that the *Penny Arcade* CPM is normally discounted lower than $5.50, as video game firms seem to buy advertising from that site in bulk (which is also likely the reason for the higher rate).

* Business Takeaway – Always keep in mind, the more targeted your site, the more distinct the demographic, the higher your potential advertising rate. "General audience" sites get the worst advertising rates. While the size of the its traffic helps, it is the desirable and targeted video game and computer enthusiast demographic that makes Penny Arcade's rates so much higher than other online comics. Always consider audience segmentation when planning your online offerings.

There is currently a legitimate academic debate, as argued by Henry Jenkins in the *MIT Technology Review* (Jenkins, "Selling Content Online") and Clay Shirky on the "Networks, Economics, and Culure" mailing list (Shirky) over the merits of banner advertising versus micropayments. Micropayments, in the context of this debate, are analogous to the established model of subscription mentioned by Hanson and Ward & Eriksen, as it is a user-based transaction like a subscription, with its innovation coming in a smaller transaction amount for a more limited, usually single use, license. Indeed, it is the epitome of Hanson's "pay-per-use."

Micropayments, as noted by Jenkins and Shirky, are currently being pioneered by a company named BitPass. BitPass takes a 15% commission for the use of its service and passes 85% of the consumer's micropayment price to the Web cartoonist, or Web company.

While we can directly compare the value of a single micropayment and a single banner ad exposure, Shirky points out that not every person who will view a Web comic funded in a provider-based model (effectively free to the viewer), will be inclined to switch to the user-based model and pay the micropayment fee (Shirky).

While data is not currently available on the conversion rate (yield) of free viewers to paid viewers, it is appropriate to account for this phenomenon by dividing the revenues and determining what percentage of provider-based viewers would need to switch to paid viewers for the two revenue models to be of equal worth. Price levels for micropayments will be based on current advertised prices by members of the BitPass program, and on prices McCloud has used as benchmarks in his books and interviews. For real world comparison, pending actual web-comics-specific data, we will default to a study of conversion rates for online newspapers, which also includes Salon.com. Salon may be a better example as it is original online material, but the results for all publications were the same: converting a previously free online to subscription or fee-based yielded an average of 1% of the "free" readers (Crosbie 2002).

Scott McCloud, who is a shareholder in BitPass, has offered 2 installments of his Flash-based graphic novel, *The Right Number.* In 7 months, McCloud has sold 2,310 copies of the first installment, and in 32 days, 797 copies of the second installment, each priced at 25 cents. A handful of other strips have started to use BitPass and micropayments as part of their revenue model, but McCloud has used it the longest, and has had the most publicity, given his status as a thought leader and academic in both the worlds of comic books and new media (Private Interview).

The implementation of micropayments, in and of itself, is controversial within the web comics community, as well as in the academic sphere. Jon Rosenberg, partially echoing Shirky's argument, has concerns about two issues related to the use of micropayments: loss of potential merchandise purchasers and no way to attract new readers if the entire strip is behind a micropayment gateway (Private Interview). McCloud concedes the second issue with no argument. In fact, he goes as far as to say that micropayments are inappropriate for the front page of a daily comic strip format. It is an accepted conclusion that readers need to be able to get a taste of a comic, print or web, before they spend money on a new product. McCloud has a free sample of the first installment of *The Right Number* available for pre-purchase browsing. The merchandising argument is a more strenuous one, as while McCloud does advocate the use of micropayments for side-promotions on daily strips, which might include a merchandising component; he is not a huge proponent of micropayments for this particular format. (Private Interview) The best use of micropayments seems to be for collections of content or comics that have a single point of download, but the equivalent of multiple pages of content, such as McCloud's *The Right Number* – a single Flash-enabled page that would easily be the equivalent of 18 printed pages, but there would be no way to put 15 ads in its formatting.

Subscription can really be broken into 2 components: magazine-style subscriptions and "premium memberships." "Premium memberships" are offered by sites like Keenspot and *Goats*. The benefits vary, but may include special content available only to subscribers, advertising-free viewing of content, and discounts on purchase of merchandise.

Modern Tales is the name brand for original web comics by subscription, with 4300 subscription spread amongst its eight sites. Some sites are anthologies, some are single-feature. Depending on the site and number of subscriptions within the system, a month of a Modern Tales family site will cost either $2.95 or $1.95. Modern Tales owner Joey Manley, while agreeing with the underlying principle behind micropayments as a method of paying for content, feels strongly that getting a one year subscription is preferable to trying to elicit a new sale each time a viewer returns to the site (Manley).

Premium memberships operate on a much smaller scale. *Goats* has 250 subscribers who pay $20 annually for a premium membership or $60 for a "super-premium" membership. Chris Crosby describes Keenspot's premium subscribers as being "in the high triple digits" for a service available for $4.95 a month or $44.95 per year (Crosby).

These rates and subscriber numbers would almost certainly put Modern Tales (as a network) and Keenspot in 5 figures for subscription income and could put *Goats* there, as well, dependent on the percentage of "super-premium" subscribers.

A tangent off of both subscriptions and micropayments that bears a cursory look is that of donations. Not considered the soundest means of generating revenue, it does have some anecdotes. Jon Rosenberg reports that for the better part of a year, *Goats* took in $750 to $1000 per month in donations running a sort of web-telethon for the strip promising a special "Sunday strip" if they met their donation goals. This worked quite well until the first month that the goal was not met. People become upset they had donated and the Sunday strip didn't appear. Donations fizzled out after that. Interestingly, Rosenberg notes that most people gave $5, even though the default value was set lower. He has hypothesized that the secret to transactions on the web is not so much the barrier of price, as it is the barrier to purchase or donate. Once you've convinced them to make a transaction, the amount has not been a delimiting factor in his experience (Private Interview).

Echoing this sentiment is Dave Anez of *BobandGeorge.com*, who says "Donations are few and far between, but since I rely more on advertising, it's not a problem. I've tried different donation incentive programs in the past, and they never really worked. The only time donations really came in handy is when the site was in serious trouble and I actually asked for help; the fans sent in over $1000 that month, but because of that, I'm reluctant to ask them for any more" (Anez).

Scott McCloud, reports that donations, his primary non-micropayment revenue stream, account for around 20% of his web income: however, given that McCloud's estimate for the last seven months is just under $1,000, donations have not been a huge revenue stream for him. In fairness, McCloud's implementation is penny-votes for the title of his "Morning Improv" series of web comics, and not part of a larger initiative.

While no longer detailed on his web site, in the early Fall of 2003, Pete Abrams of *Sluggy Freelance* posted a plea for people to support the strip and buy some merchandise or he might have to devote less time to the strip. That request could be considered similar to Anez's experience, as the results were apparently to Abrams' satisfaction and the plea hasn't been repeating... at least not in the approximate six months between the request and this writing.

These stories, which seem typical of the experience are enough to form a hypothesis that donations can be an effective emergency measure if a web comic has developed a following and there is a demonstrable crisis at hand. Donations have not, however, proved themselves to be a reliable revenue stream in the long term, and while worth a mention, will be discarded from the analysis.

The final revenue stream is merchandising. This is the packaging and licensing of real world goods based on the web comic. This can include t-shirts, buttons, stickers, stuffed animals. For the definitions of this thesis, it will also include the printed editions of the web comics, as they are not the original format and have become a revenue stream separate from the web incarnation of the comics.

It is important to recognize that web merchandising is very idiosyncratic. Not every web comic is equally well suited for a stuffed animal. Some art styles may not lend themselves to t-shirts as well as others. As has been mentioned specifically in the case of Scott McCloud, some web comics are not meant to be collected in print.

Two of the biggest proponents of merchandising as a revenue stream are Jon Rosenberg of *Goats* and R Stevens of *Diesel Sweeties*. Both have given up on advertising in favor of merchandising. Stevens takes merchandising a step further and has a merchandise subscription. His "Clango Club" is essentially "a subscription service which uses a recurring Paypal payment to charge $5 per month from a user in exchange for stickers, buttons, extra comics, etc. on a mostly monthly basis." Stevens places his subscriber base at around 200 and his average number of daily visitors around 20,000 (R Stevens). This would put his number of number of subscribers at 1% - the same number Crosbie quotes for converting free users to paid users for online newspapers.

*Business Takeaway – When projecting any type of conversion from a web site, 1% is the magic number. You may get a higher number with a more targeted audience, but everyone's average conversion – free to paid/subscriber or web viewer to purchaser – revolves around a 1% conversion.

Rosenberg agrees with using 1% as a rule of thumb for how many of a web comic's audience will buy merchandise, emphasizing it as the reason he views micropayments as a failure. Rosenberg has found great success selling t-shirts. A recent riff on Harry Potter's arch foe resulted in the "Republicans for Voldemort" which quickly sold over 1,000 shirts. Other shirts sell around half that. Rosenberg muses that, in a way, he's created a t-shirt store that's sponsored by a comic strip, and one of his challenges as a designer is to create shirts that, while retaining some connection to the strip, are still hip and entertaining to someone who's never seen Goats (Private Interview). That seems to be a valid way to look at it, and is indeed antithetical to McCloud's notion of paying for the ability to read digital comics.

Rosenberg raves that he has been able to make five times as much off his merchandising as off his subscriptions and that advertising doesn't come close to generating the revenue he gets off t-shirts, noting a profit margin of up to 50%, which would be as much as $9 per item in some cases. Stevens quotes $4-$5 as his margin. Rosenberg further claims to have tripled his 2003 income by switching to t-shirt sales in the last three months of 2003.

Chris Crosby of Keenspot re-emphasizes that merchandising varies heavily from web comic to web comic, and running a site with over 50 features would give him some perspective on this. Stating that some features lend themselves better to plush toys (Crosby currently sells two stuffed toys from Keenspot features) and t-shirts, he sums it up by saying, "Generally, you can count on at least 0.5% of your readership buying stuff, if the stuff is at all appealing (and that can be tricky for some cartoonists). But it all depends on lots of factors." In general he sees no reason, if the combination of audience and design are correct, not to equal or exceed advertising revenues with merchandising.

Looking past the t-shirts, back to books, there seems to be a consensus that books are more for the hardcore fan of a comic and t-shirts can find a wider audience outside the normal audience. Books come along slowly, as material accumulates, while t-shirts are deployed more rapidly. Rosenberg and Stevens both speak of "retiring" shirts and moving on to new designs.

While merchandising may not be for every strip, it has the potential to supplant (or supplement) other revenue models.

*Business Takeaway – If your content lends itself to merchandising, particularly with a healthy margin, and you wish to make that a primary revenue stream, it is more important for people to see your content than it is to directly pay for it. If 1% of the audience will pay for online content, then 99% of the potential audience for your merchandising will not see your content. You can't have it both ways.

The real wild card in calculating the revenues of web comics is the cost of bandwidth. The size of a web comic tends to be very much a personal thing with anything going from a black and white replication of a daily newspaper comic strip to a comic-book sized full color page. The cost of bandwidth also varies widely – to the extent, once a beginner account is passed, there is no rhyme or reason to hosting costs. It all boils down to what kind of a deal can be negotiated.

The graphic for a black and white comic strip formatted web comic, roughly 670 pixels x 275 pixels, will be in the neighborhood of 30K in size. A full color comic book page (600 pixels by 875 pixels) could be 500K or more in size. Additionally, many web comics have a great deal of text on the page with advertising copy, links, logos and the like and adding as much as an additional 100K to the page.

* Business Takeaway – Web design manuals will talk about how large the file size of a page should be, in terms of downloading quickly. This is relevant, however, as a businessman you should also be concerned how large a page's download size is, because you're ultimately paying for the amount a data transferred. As your traffic increases, this becomes increasingly important, so get in the mindset of conserving bandwidth now, and always determine

what your cost to serve a webpage is in relationship to the income off a page. It may sound obvious, but it is seldom emphasized.

A basic hosting package will normally cost about $10 and include perhaps 10 gigs of transfer. Valueweb.com offers 1000 GB of data transfer for $59 per month, although the extras, including merchant account, would drive the cost closer to $100. (Value Web) 1000 GB would account for approximately 7.5 million pageviews of a 30K web comic with 100K of other material on the page. For a larger strip of 150K (the largest size you'll find in most web comics) with 100K of extra material per page, such an account would account for 4 million page views. Such an account would satisfy all but the top few web comics.

Still, off the record, you hear of web cartoonists paying $800 - $1000 per month for large amounts of data transfer or dedicated connections.

First, it is appropriate to take a look at raw levels of income from advertising. Along the top of the following table are CPM rates that have been mentioned ($3.50 is listed as a potential discount off of an advertised $5.50 CPM); along the left hand side of the chart are benchmark monthly page views with certain web comics attached as appropriate. Please note that the $0.40 CPM is an approximation of giving up 50% of the banner rate to a banner ad network, should one be used.

	$0.16	$0.40	$0.85	$1.00
70 M. (Keenspot)	$11,200	$28,000	$59,500	$70,000
29 M. (Penny Arcade)	$4,640	$11,600	$24,650	$29,000
9 M. (PVP)	$1,440	$3,600	$7,650	$9,000
6 M.(Sexy Losers)	$960	$2400	$5,100	$6,000

5 M. (Sinfest / Real Life)	$800	$2,000	$4,250	$5,000
1.5 M. (Goats / Bob and George)	$240	$600	$1,275	$1,500
500K	$80	$200	$425	$500
100K	$16	$40	$85	$100

	$1.50	$3.50	$5.50
70 M. (Keenspot)	$105,000	$245,000	$385,000
29 M. (Penny Arcade)	$43,500	$101,500	$159,500
9 M. (PVP)	$13,500	$31,500	$49,500
6 M.(Sexy Losers)	$9,000	$21,000	$33,000
5 M. (Sinfest / Real Life)	$7,500	$17,500	$27,500
1.5 M. (Goats / Bob and George)	$2,250	$5,250	$8,250
500K	$750	$1,750	$2,750
100K	$150	$350	$550

It becomes quickly apparent that should a large web comic really cost in the range of $800 - $1000 to host, should strips be relying on half of a banner network rate to pay for a dedicated connection, it would not be enough money. On the other hand, *Penny Arcade*, which employs 2 banners could be pulling in $200,000 - $300,000 from advertising each month, depending on inventory sell-through and potential discounting.

Comparing micropayments to banner ads is important when making a decision between the two. BitPass charges a 15% commission, so the following chart translates the retail price of a micropayment into the effective CPM of the system. While not currently technically feasible, McCloud has long spoken of the possibility of charging half a cent for a daily comic strip, so that price has been included for theoretical examination. [(Price)(85% of price retained)(1000 purchases)]

Retail Price	Cartoonist's Share	Effective CPM
$0.50	$0.425	$425.00
$0.25	$0.2125	$212.50
$0.10	$0.085	$85.00
$0.05	$0.0425	$42.50
$0.01	$0.0085	$8.50
$0.005	$0.00425	$4.25

Comparing the value of 1000 micropayment purchasers to 1000 viewers, it is possible to determine the acceptable traffic losses while retaining the same level of revenue. Micropayment prices are along left hand side of the chart and advertising CPM's are across the top of the chart. Taking Crosbie's 1% conversion rule into account, anytime a micropayment price point would yield the same revenue with a 1% or less retention (99% or greater traffic loss), the box has been shaded to indicate a micropayment would theoretically generate equal or greater revenue in that comparison.

	$0.16	$0.40	$0.85	$1.00	$1.50	$3.50	$5.50
$0.50 ($425 CPM)	99.9%	99.9%	99.8%	99.8%	99.6%	99.2%	98.7%
$0.25 ($212.50 CPM)	99.9%	99.8%	99.6%	99.5%	99.3%	98.4%	97.4%
$0.10 ($85 CPM)	99.8%	99.5%	99%	98.8%	98.2%	95.9%	93.5%
$0.05 ($42.50 CPM)	99.6%	99.1%	98%	97.6%	96.5%	91.7%	87.1%
$0.01 ($8.50 CPM)	98.1%	95.3%	90%	88.2%	82.4%	58.8%	35.3%
$0.005 ($4.25 CPM)	96.2%	90.5%	80%	76.5%	64.7%	17.6%	TOTAL LOSS

As the acceptable traffic loss chart illustrates, even with a banner network CPM of $0.16 or $0.40 for the equivalent amount of materials, the micropayment would have to be five cents for there to be any gross revenue benefit. If the micropayment were for a week's worth of web comics, say the equivalent of five pages of an advertising based site, the comparative CPM multiplies by the five instances being traded against a single micropayment (for example, a $0.40 CPM with 5 exposures becomes a $2 CPM) and the shaded area of benefit slides further to the left.

For comparison, let's convert *The Right Number* into comic book pages. This is an inexact science, but good for illustration. McCloud estimates that one installment of *The Right Number*, should it be placed in a conventional format, would take up about 18 comic book sized pages. If we assume Crosbie's 1% is in effect, so if *The Right Number*'s first installment had 2,310 purchases, it should have had in the neighborhood of 231,000 readers, were it free to view, and at 18 pages per viewer, that would be a total of 4,158,000 pageviews for the installment. Applying the standard range of CPM rates, it is possible to project *The Right Number's* potential advertising income as the following:

$0.16	$0.40	$0.85	$1.00	$1.50	$3.50	$5.50
$665.28	$1,663.20	$3,534.30	$4,158	$6,237	$14,553	$22,869

Giving BitPass a 15% commission off of a $0.25 micropayment would give McCloud roughly $490 for the first installment. Dependent on McCloud's demographics being targeted to a specific niche, it is most likely he would fall somewhere between $0.16 CPM and $0.85 CPM as a general audience site. Should Crosbie's 1% rule hold, McCloud would likely double his gross revenues by switching to standard advertising. In fairness, it should be noted that McCloud's intent is to make a revenue model fit the art form, and not vice versa.

Merchandising is hard to quantify, past that t-shirts seem to be the most popular and accessible item. Assuming a merchandise purchasing conversion rate of 1%, 100 readers will yield 1 customer. If a web comic runs 5 days per week, if a new product is introduced each month, then ads for [(readers) (comics per week) (4 weeks/month)]

2000 pageviews = 1 shirt sold.
(1200 pageviews = 1 shirt, if 3x per week)
(2000 page views) ($0.85 CPM) = $1.70
1 T-shirt = $9

Merchandising, in this scenario, would be 5.3x as profitable as advertising.

The following chart shows the effective CPM of a piece of merchandise based on a set product margin, contrasted with a hypothetical conversion rate and the number of strips appearing per week. The chart is based on a one month period and accounts for the 1% conversion rate endorsed by Rosenberg and Crosbie, as well as the worst-case scenario 0.5% suggested by Crosby.

[(conversion rate)(1000 readers)(product margin) / (1000 reader) (number of comics per week) (4 weeks in a month) = effective CPM]

	1% conversion - @3/week	1% conversion - @5/week	0.5% conversion - @3/week	0.5% conversion - @5/week
$9 margin	$7.50	$4.50	$3.75	$2.25
$5 margin	$4.17	$2.50	$2.08	$1.25
$3 margin	$2.50	$1.50	$1.25	$0.75
$1 margin	$0.83	$0.50	$0.42	$0.25

Mathematics say, should the theory hold and the cartoonist can produce an attractive product with at least a $5 margin, the site should be at least as well off with merchandising as it is with advertising, unless it has a particularly desirable demographic (e.g., Penny Arcade and, most likely, PVP). Sites with worse luck obtaining high CPM rates could conceivably be better off selling an item with a $1 margin, but such trade-offs would require close monitoring.

* Business Takeaway – Always analyze and compare the effectiveness of your revenue streams. And remember, you can use more than one. If your primary audience is micropayments or subscription, you may still sell some merchandise. Just not as much.

Factoring the cost of hosting into the revenue stream is tricky. The price structure of a hosting contract generally takes three forms. The first form is a contract with a fixed amount of bandwidth transfer allotted. Should the amount of data transferred exceed the contracted amount, the website would shut down. The second type of contract includes a fixed amount of bandwidth and any excess amount of bandwidth is charged as it used, usually at price between $2 and $6 per gigabyte. Each of the two types of contracts comes with a danger to the website owner. If data transfer is exceeded, which could be an indication that the site is being successful, the site could either be shut down or incur a sizeable bill for the increased traffic that might exceed the ability of the web cartoonist to pay.

The third type of contract is one where a bandwidth connection is leased, not an amount of transfer. With this method a "pipe" is established, often a one megabyte per second connection, and all data flows unmetered through that connection. Should traffic demand be higher than the pipe capacity, the website would not shut down, so much as the viewers would find the download very slow, although in extreme cases, it might cause a shut down. (Certain hacker tactics involve overloading a server with webpage and data requests, for example.)

Prices on these contracts vary widely. The basic starter contract is approximately $10 per month and typically will include somewhere between 10 GB and 30 GB of data transfer. Past that there is no rhyme or reason to pricing. Off the record comments from web cartoonists range from $200 for 600 GB transfer to between $750 and $1000 for a dedicated connection.

Larger sites like *Penny Arcade* or *PVP* may have the ability to trade in some publicity and/or endorsement to reduce their hosting rate, and you see certain web comics linking to their hosting firms. Still, the posted numbers on hosting company sites seldom match up with the numbers reported by web cartoonists, as negotiation is the way of life for larger contracts.

A reasonable rule of thumb is to estimate $3 per GB of transfer, but $100, $200 and $1000 are all reasonable estimates for hosting costs. It is simply the nature of the business. Modern Tales owner Joey Manley is jumping into the hosting game with webcomicsnation.com and will be offering professional accounts with "unmetered" bandwidth transfer and an impressive number of features geared towards content publishing and web comics, including an e-commerce system. It is not known what level of bandwidth transfer will cause a renegotiation of terms, but that is likely to occur at some point, but the advantage of an "unmetered" account is there will not be a sudden extra bill from a surge in traffic.

* Business Takeaway – When pricing and planning your hosting, make sure you know the possible solutions and penalties should a surge in popularity take you past your plan's bandwidth limits. Getting caught unprepared can be expensive.

Chapter 6A: Downloads March On and Micropayments Change

The music industry has been transformed by the paid download. 2006 is the year that paid downloads of comics started to gain momentum in the United States. There have been several experiments over the years.

The first paid downloads to gain any widespread attention were eBooks at UnboundComics.com. For $1.75 each, you could download PDF/Adobe formatted eBooks of a variety of old and out of print comics like Dalgoda and Timothy Truman's Wilderness. Unbound also featured some original content, notably early work from Ben (30 Days of Night) Templesmith, as Templesmith adapted Shakespeare's Hamlet.

Unbound was eventually folded into the eBook website Fictionwise.com. 8 eBooks remain online, thought the price has risen to $2.25.

McCloud's Experiment Fails

Scott McCloud's micropayment experiment yielded a reasonable number of downloads, but not a sustainable revenue stream for a "full-time" income. Unfortunately, things got much worse for the BitPass micropayment system.

In early June 2005, Jon Rosenberg of Goats.com ran an experiment with the BitPass micropayment system. It cannot be emphasized enough how unscientific and idiosyncratic this experiment was, but it is the first attempt of a web comic with a large circulation and revenue base in merchandising to test the micropayment system.

The promotion was putting digital editions of two of their print-based mini-comics for sale at BitPass for 25 cents each. They also allowed for a $1 discount off the print editions, should someone purchase the digital edition and wish to also purchase the print edition (both of which were priced at $4). This is an imperfect test for several reasons:

1) As one of the mini-comics being offered online had previously existed as a print product, the portion of the Goats audience most interested in supplemental material may have already purchased the print edition.

2) This is a test only of supplemental sales. The main Goats strip continued to be freely available on Goats.com. This test cannot conclusively be used for a previously free strip migrating to a pay-per-view format.

3) This event was widely covered in the online community, yielding higher traffic and theoretically more sales resulting from higher traffic.

4) Rosenberg's announcement of the proposal included a mild dose of skepticism towards micropayments may have slightly tainted the conversion rate.

The results were 213 digital mini-comics were sold in a week, for a total of $53.25, before BitPass takes their fee. A small amount of money and much less than the site normally makes off its merchandising efforts. Rosenberg reports on June 7, the heaviest day for BitPass sales, 73 mini-comics were sold and over 80,0000 people visited Goats.com. This would make for a conversion rate of less than 1/10 of a percent. Rosenberg had previously estimated a conversion rate of closer to 1% for his site.

More disturbingly, the BitPass promotion coincided with overall sales on his site tanking.

"When [Penny Arcade] linked to us last June we had our best month ever," Rosenberg reports on his website. "Despite a larger regular audience and a link from that same site we are on track to sell approximately 3/10 as much this month over the year before."

He goes on to detail the sale of only 2 copies of the paper edition of his new mini-comic in that time period.

Can the drop in merchandising revenues be directly linked to BitPass? That's a subject for debate. Rosenberg sticks by his theory that as long as the price of an item is under $20, price is not a barrier to purchase for his web comic, rather the initiative of the consumer to complete a transaction is the real barrier. By this reasoning, the consumer attention was focused on a 25 cent transaction, instead of an $18 transaction. He also cites the bus pass-like nature of BitPass as a problem, with potential customers needing to purchase a $3 account from BitPass to purchase a 25 cent comic. The issue of the unspent $2.75 in the BitPass system is a topic of venomous debate on the Goats message boards, and while message boards are a self-selected sample, it does confirm the issue is real, if not the extent to which it is a barrier.

While this experiment is somewhat anecdotal, it does suggest that merchandising does not mix well for a pay-per-view strip, and that established web comics with a mix of revenue streams should approach a move to micropayments with caution, especially if they plan on keeping part of their content freely available on their original site.

In January 2007, BitPass went out of business. Perhaps not coincidentally, in late 2005, online payment processor, PayPal, announced a new discount structure for micropayments: transactions under $2.00 cost $.05 plus 5% of the transaction. While not as efficient as BitPass was a processor with very small amounts as a quarter, this program is a vast improvement for consumers and makes iTune-style $0.99 downloads much more feasible.

An Expensive Download

Moving forward to February 2006, another download experiment began, one with a bit more data available, as your author was in charge of the implementation. *The Flying Friar* was a one-shot graphic novella possibly best known at the time of solicitation for its author, Rich Johnston. Johnston is best known for the long-running gossip column "Lying in the Gutters" at ComicBookResources.com, and though he has dabbled in comics several times over the years, was not really known for his comics work at this point. Initial orders for the book were estimated at 1700.

A week before book was released, a minor media storm hit. *The Flying Friar* was a satire combining the myth of Superman with St. Joseph of Copertino, an actual Catholic saint. The book was covered by the *Times of London, The Guardian,* BBC radio and papers as far away as Italy and India. In the face of a sudden swarm of publicity, it was decided to co-opt the RichJohnston.com website into a download site for a PDF version of *The Flying Friar.* As the download was to be launched the Sunday after the book was released in print, the price was set at the same as the cover price, $4.95, in an effort to reduce channel conflict and promote the download as an alternative to the print edition. Unfortunately, the site was launched after the initial mainstream coverage and was discussed almost exclusively on comic book web sites.

The response was successful more from a systemic sense, than raw numbers. In the following year, 44 copies were downloaded. A small number, but not necessarily when looked at in context. 1% is the rule of thumb number when figuring conversions. 44 copies translate to a little over 2.5% of the print orders. Additionally, the conversion rate for incoming visitors was 2%. Both numbers being double what you would expect for a one-off website of a small press product, especially when deal with an audience known for collecting printed comics. Perhaps more in line with expectations in an international marketplace, 23% of downloads were confirmed as foreign. Perhaps the largest difference would be in the revenue. 213 copies of Goats for $0.25 yield a gross revenue of $53.25. 44 copies of the Flying Friar is $217.80.

As a test case, this shows a slightly greater than expected market proportional the traditional print market showing up and purchasing for the print price. It also makes a case for further experiments.

Downloads For Everyone

The end of 2006 saw three new players entering this paid download space:

- Eyemelt.com, the online effort of print publisher, Slave Labor Graphics. As of this writing, Eyemelt is only selling digital edition of Slave Labor comics, but has started running two series that are original to the web. Downloads that were previously in print cost $0.69, while original downloads are priced at $0.89.
- Pullboxonline.com, an online effort by the staff of Devil's Due. At the time of this writing, Pullboxonline.com is primarily offering downloads of comics by Devil's Due, along with a smaller

selection of IDW titles, three downloads by cartoonist Jim Mahfood, and "Night Club," a mini-series that appeared under the Image logo in 2005. Most downloads are priced at $0.99, up to $4.99 for a graphic novel.

- Drivethrucomics.com, an eBook store/spinoff by online role playing games retailer, Drivethrurpg.com. Drivethrucomics.com offers most downloads for $1.99, though a digital edition of a graphic novel can be as high as $11.95. Drivethrucomics offers both old and current comics by a variety of publishers, but no original works.

This download model is still very young, and there just isn't enough data available to draw absolute rule on the format's behavior, but with some information shared by Eyemelt's Dan Vado and DriveThruComics.com's Scott Wieck, we can make some observations.

Observation #1: There is an audience, we just don't know the size. Everyone emphasizes that comic downloads are a young medium and these things take a year or two to grow into an independent market. At this point is appropriate to remember that iTunes also started slowly. Vado suspects the 2%-2.5% ratio of print circulation to paid down on *The Flying Friar* will prove an accurate figure. Wieck offers that his firm has found that digital downloads account for **11%** of role playing games sales. He reports top sellers for DriveThruComics.com range range from 600-800 copies. (It should also note that site is integrated with a large role playing game side and has an existing, and purchasing, audience). Suffice it to say, there appears to be room to grow.

Observation #2: Price is not set. With a range of $0.69 all the way up to cover price, the market has not settled on a price point yet.

Observation #3: Format is not set. Currently, we're seeing downloads offered in either a .PDF or a .CBR format. .CBR being the format commonly used for pirated scans of comics on BitTorrent streams. Yes, we may have a case of piracy creating demand. Whether this will become a Tower of Babel situation with too many reader formats splintering the market, as is often complained about in prose eBook circles, remains to be seen.

Observation #4: PayPal is a tool for this market. Eyemelt.com uses PayPal, and reports users typical purchase downloads individually, regardless of the total number of titles purchased on a site visit. DriveThruComics.com uses PayPal in conjunction with a traditional credit card processing service. This would be a micropayment market BitPass missed out on, and the ability to use a credit card for a single purchase would seem to be a driving reason.

Observation #5: All types of content are selling. DriveThruComics.com reports most of their top selling titles are tied to a licensed property, but questions whether or not there's enough data to be conclusive. Devil's Due reports their non-licensed properties do better and they've been surprised by some of their older titles. Eyemelt.com says "the two downloadable only series we have are far and away outstripping sales of [comics that are] only in print." That is unexpected. With so many web comics available for free viewing, a reasonable expectation would be that a paid download would either have to have an established and very popular creative team, or have a print edition for sale to establish the value. In the case of *Whistles*, Eyemelt.com's initial original-for-the-web title, it was cartoonist Andrew Hussie's published first work. Perhaps it speaks to strong editorial branding from Slave Labor. Perhaps it's a similar audience to the subscribers of Modern Tales. Perhaps it's a statistical anomaly. In any case, we can say that original content is not being discriminated against, thus far.

Observation #5: Web-to-Print Is Still Part of This Model. Vado will be collecting the original-for-web comics and printing them as trade paperbacks. Just as the freely viewed web comics have spawned print editions, this is planned here as well. It makes the same amount of sense as the freely-viewed web comics selling collections. After all, Spider-Man and Batman have plenty of collected edition books. Also, as a print publisher, Vado already has a pipeline into the direct market, which most web cartoonists do not.

* Business Takeaway: Keep watching. This is a developing trend and will likely be the most palatable to existing print publishers, if the initial observations bear out. Web comics could use a definitive portal, like iTunes, to centralize an audience. Darwinism will eventually cause this through a combination of audience migrations and buy-outs.

Chapter 6B: Advertising Surges

Advertising markets always fluctuate, and 2007 has started out to be a good year for banner advertisements. Accordingly, more web comics are taking advantage of it.

Penny Arcade, a site that has always counted advertising as a cornerstone of its revenue model reports that rates are now in the $5-$9 CPM range, up from $5-$5.50 in 2005. Remember that Penny Arcade typically runs 2 ads on its homepage and factor in that their traffic has risen to approach 55 million page views per month. While 55 million page views likely include their sans-advertising message board, this is an excellent illustration of advertising's potential as a revenue stream. Penny Arcade is in a special situation, having a viewer demographic that tightly fits the advertising need of the video game industry and may well have the highest CPMs in web comics. They also sell their own ads, which is not always the case.

There are three mechanisms by which a web comic will source advertising:
- Selling it on their own
- Sourcing it from an advertising network
- Automated contextual advertising

Selling it on their own is commonly thought of as the best method, given sufficient traffic and resources to justify a full-time or part-time salesman. MegaTokyo, for instance, still offers their banners for a $1.60 CPM off their own site.

Advertising networks are the most common method used by websites, outside of web comics. They work in two ways, selling both advertising targeted at a specific web site and "run of network" advertising that is spread freely through all members of the network, usually constrained only by broad content categories like "entertainment" or "business." Targeted advertising pays more, and mainstream advertising networks typically take 40-50% of the advertising rate as their fee.

Advertising networks did not typically accept web comics until relatively recently. Now a few instances are starting to appear. The IndieClick(.com) network appears on strips like Goats and Diesel Sweeties, for example.

More commonly, a group of strips will be represented as a single entity, creating an advertising network for collective use. Keenspot, while conceived as a host, is also an advertising network for the features under its umbrella. Blank Label Comics is another group of strips operating as their own network. Interestingly, Blank Lablel was started by cartoonists leaving the Keenspot Network.

Another variation on the network is "Project Wonderful"(.com), which encourages advertisers to make daily bids on individual sites. The rates vary widely, and the site is too new to judge, but some sites do appear to be experiencing some initial success.

Contextual advertising, commonly referred to as "Google Ads" after the program that popularized the format, are ads that are served based on the content of a given web page. Specifically the text of a page. Ads are bid on, based on key words and phrases and if the same word or phrase appears on a web page, the ad is served. Payment occurs only if a viewer clicks on this ad. Contextual advertising is best known as the predominant form of advertising found on blogs.

The problem contextual advertising presents to web comics is that the computer program the controls which ads go on a page makes ad placement decisions based on text, whereas the main content for a web comic is graphic in nature. This has been alleviated, to an extent, by including text transcripts underneath the comics.

This can cause some odd ad placement. For instance, a visit to the web comic Schlock Mercenary(.com) finds contextual ads for "Utah Massage College" and "Utah Divorce Lawyer." Why are these ads there? Cartoonist Howard Tayler lives in Utah, and the state occasionally shows up in the text of the site. (By all accounts, Howard is happily married and not looking for a divorce lawyer.)

One reason web cartoonists use contextual advertising is the ease of entry into a program. Banner networks have historically been hesitant to represent web comics and also have minimum page view requirements that would rule out comics just starting out. With most contextual program, you sign up, insert some code onto your homepage, and you're off to the races.

It should also be noted that at least one contextual network, Google Adwords, gives the option for an advertiser to target a specific website. Under such a scenario, Google functions much like a traditional ad network, with the exception being the advertiser found the individual website in question, the site was not being marketed before the point of sale.

While many sites will stick with one advertising network, others don't. Some networks may stipulate exclusivity, but Schlock Mercenary features ads from Google, BlogAds(.com) and Blank Label. Proprietor Tayler says the revenue from each stream varies from month-to-month, each having their moment in the sun.

While contextual advertising is definitely a case-by-case proposition, here are some published advertising rates from February 2007, converted to CPM:

Blank Label Comics: $0.50 - $1.00 CPM
KeenSpot: $1.00 CPM
MegaTokyo: $1.60 CPM

Penny Arcade: $5 - $9 CPM

***Business Takeaway: Advertising has emerged as a viable revenue stream for consideration in your overall mix. Be sure to investigate opportunities with an established non-comics-specific advertising network when your traffic is high enough to qualify.
Contextual ads with Google or Yahoo are a perfectly acceptable start, and the only way to gauge their value to your individual content is through experimentation.**

Chapter 6C – Diversifying Revenue

As web comics have evolved, so has the use of a hybrid revenue model. Fewer sites rely on a single revenue stream and some use several.

Penny Arcade, one of the innovators in business practices from online comics, has five separate revenue streams:

- Advertising
- Merchandising (including their publishing efforts)
- Commissioned work (often specialty comic strips for other sites or games)
- Brand Consulting
- PAX – The Penny Arcade eXpo. From their website: "PAX is a three-day game festival for tabletop, videogame, and PC gamers." Yes, Penny Arcade runs a consumer convention for video games.

No, most websites don't run a convention, but Penny Arcade is a high-end example. Business Director Robert Khoo reports that no single revenue stream accounts for more than 40% of their earnings. Remember, in Chapter 5B, Khoo also reported CPMs of $5-$9 and 55 million monthly page views. This adds up to Penny Arcade being a multi-million dollar business. Penny Arcade has gotten large enough that the use of a third-party fulfillment operation no longer makes fiscal sense, so they will be opening their own warehouse for merchandise fulfillment.

PVP, another top-tier strip, started a subscription-based cartoon based on the strip available at the website, in February 2007, and is one of the first web comics to be syndicated on cell phones (though it's the Image comic book version being used for the cell phone edition).

Schlock Mercenary's Howard Tayler, who previously discussed his diversification of advertising sources and book sales, averages a revenue split of 80% merchandising income to 20% advertising income.

Goats, which was originally excluding advertising, in favor of merchandising, has since added a banner network to the mix and put premium subscriptions on hold.

Modern Tales (.com) has opened a section of content that is freely viewed and advertising-supported on their suite of sites, as well as expanding into the paid hosting business with WebComicsNation (.com), which also utilizes advertising for part of its revenue stream. This is notable, in that as print publisher start moving towards paid downloads, the original paid content site for comics is opening up to free include viewing, ad-supported models.

And flipping that over, Eyemelt(.com)'s Dan Vado intends to collect his original online titles in print editions for a secondary stream in the near future.

*Business Takeaway – The current trend is to balance your income with multiple streams. This is especially wise in the case of advertising. By its nature, advertising rates will rise and fall with outside economic factors.

*Business Takeaway – Increasingly, the end product of a web comic is a graphic novel or printed collected edition. This is no different from someone reading Calvin & Hobbes or Garfield in the newspaper and buying a collected edition of that. It still holds true for downloading digital copies of print monthlies. Digital reading will breed collectors who want a print copy and will pay for it. This end product need not be the only revenue stream cultivated.

Chapter 7: Web Vs. Print

Looking at the respective revenue models, it is fair to ask if it is better to do a printed comic or a web comic.

The obvious answer is that at lower circulation levels, the advantage is with web comics, since a web comic can start from a $10 account and earn revenue immediately, while the economics of print dictate a minimum circulation, which may be difficult to achieve for the beginner. With the web, the cartoonist has the luxury of building audience.

Scott McCloud is a good example of this. *The Right Number* is essentially a serialized digital graphic novel, much as an increasing number of print comics are serials that become collected as a graphic novel. Online, the first installment of *The Right Number* sold 2310 copies over a period of 7 months. At a download size of 1.63 MB, a $10 beginner hosting account would be able to handle over 6000 such downloads in a given month, so it is relatively safe to count his total materials cost for the period at $70. As previously calculated, after BitPass takes its share, McCloud's revenues for this installment would have been approximately $490, leaving him with a net revenue of $420 after hosting costs. [This will not be 100% accurate, as McCloud continues to host his "Morning Improv" web comic on the same site, which may push him into a higher bandwidth category, and there are small samples available that would incrementally increase the cost, but this demonstrates the ability of micropayments to reduce bandwidth costs while retaining income.] Should McCloud have released this as a print comic, his initial order would likely not have been enough to break even on printing, were he to publish it himself, and paying a 10% royalty for 2300 copies, should someone else publish it would hit right around the point of breaking even for the publisher. Clearly, for small projects, the web has the advantage.

More practically, let us create a comparison chart for web strips with circulation levels of 9 million, 5 million, 1.5 million, 500,000 and 100,000 pageviews respectively. These shall be measured by the CPM ranges used previously less $2000 for hosting for the 9 million pageview site (estimating 2 connection lines leased at $1000), $1000 for the 5 million pageview site (one leased connection line), $300 for the 1.5 million and 500,000 pageview sites (estimating on the high end for a 600 – 700 GB account) and $100 for the 100,000 pageview account (this site could potentially fall into a $10 hosting account, depending on exact page sizes and the hosting contract, but this will be a conservative estimate).

	$0.16	$0.40	$0.85	$1	$1.5	$3.5
9 Million	($560)	$1600	$5650	$7000	$11,500	$29,500
5 Million	($200)	$1000	$3250	$4000	$6500	$16,500
1.5 Million	($60)	$300	$975	$1200	$1950	$4950
500,000	($220)	($100)	$125	$200	$450	$1450
100,000	($84)	($60)	($15)	$0	$50	$250

The first thing you notice is how hard it is to turn a profit off a $0.16 CPM. If more $100 accounts are available, then the red numbers slide to the right significantly. There is a gap between when a web comic exits a beginner account and hits around 1 million page views per month, in terms of affordability of bandwidth, unless a special hosting package is negotiated.

Based strictly on advertising, the 1.5 million pageview level is where advertising starts to become effective at the sample rates. Around one million pageviews is also the threshold of size for corporate ad buying (something best exploited by strips with strong, targeted demographics like *Penny Arcade*). At this level, an $0.85 CPM is slightly more than a 10% royalty on a $2.95 print comic book with a 3,000 copy circulation, and a $1.25 CPM would approximately equal the entire estimated revenue for a 3,000 print run comic book. At 5 million page views, a $1 CPM gives you more revenue than a 5,000 print run $2.95 black and white comic or an 8,000 print run $2.95 cent color comic, both very respectable sales figures in the direct market. At 9 million, a *Penny Arcade*-style CPM, as it suspected *PVP* can command, would generate more income than Marvel's creative budget.

Next, while it is not appropriate for every strip, let us add an extra $1.25 CPM to account for merchandising with a 0.5% conversion rate and $5 margin with 20 strips per month representing one reader.

	$0.16 + $1.25	$0.40 + $1.25	$0.85 + $1.25	$1 + $1.25	$1.5 + $1.25	$3.5 + $1.25
9 Million	$10,690	$12,850	$16,900	$18,250	$22,750	$40,750
5 Million	$6050	$7250	$9,500	$10,250	$12,750	$22,750
1.5 Million	$1815	$2175	$2850	$3075	$3825	$6825
500,000	$405	$525	$750	$825	$1075	$2075
100,000	$41	$65	$110	$125	$175	$375

Illustrating the power of merchandising as a revenue stream, now even the 500,000 pageview level web comic is making the equivalent royalty of 10% on a 3,000 circulation $2.95 book and the 5 million pageview web comic approaches Marvel's creative budget

If the conversion rate is really closer to 1%, the numbers jump again.

There aren't that many web comics at the 5 million or above pageview level. There are an increasing number at the 1 to 1.5 million pageview level. If the web cartoonist can make compelling merchandise on a regular basis, there seems to be a revenue advantage to being on the web, as opposed to being an independent (non- Diamond Premiere Partner-published) print comic book. At the very top of the game, revenue may equal or exceed that of the creative budget for a Marvel comic book, but for most, a Marvel contract would prove more lucrative.

At the low end, web comics, particularly micropayments, allow for experimentation and a minor amount of income, where it would not be economically realistic to print. If the web comic in question is not particularly appropriate for merchandising, then there could be greater economic benefit to direct market publishing for web comics up until around the 1.5 million download level. It should be noted, though, that this evaluation is based on materials vs. revenue, and while web comics are largely promoted through word of mouth, there may be advertising costs associated with print comics that could make independent publishing less attractive.

All this is complicated by hosting packages and the reality that it is likely the web cartoonists may need to switch not just hosting packages, but likely hosting companies as the web site's traffic grows.

This comparison does not include merchandising or book/reprint collections for print comics. While greater numbers of serial stories are collected in book format, and t-shirts, posters and the like are common spinning off from print comic books, they are not guaranteed to happen with every title and the justification for the spin-offs normally occurs after the series has had a modicum of success. In essence, merchandise spin-offs are a bonus in the print industry. As has been demonstrated here, such things are part of the business plan for many web comics.

Chapter 8: Blown to Bits?

In their book, *Blown to Bits*, Philip Evans and Thomas Wurster discuss technology's ability to undermine existing businesses by changing the paradigm an industry operates on. Their initial example is of the encyclopedia industry, which was almost crippled by its failure to react to two things: the advent of the CD-Rom and the Internet search engine. Microsoft distributed a repackaged version of the Funk and Wagnall encyclopedia on a CD-Rom, free with its other offerings and people began to look up topics on the Internet. By the time Encyclopedia Britannica responded, their company was in dire straits. Their market had been "blown to bits" (Evans & Wurster pp. 1-7).

Much of Evans & Wurster's writing concerns issues of richness, reach and disintermediation, all of which figure largely when comparing print and web comics. When Bill Jemas says he took Marvel away from the newsstand and into book reprints, he's talking about a richness and reach trade-off. Marvel lost some of its reach by retracting off the newsstands into the bookstores, but the book reprints contained richer content – the six issues of a title Jemas didn't trust a child to pluck off the magazine rack in consecutive months. A key difference with the Internet is that richness and reach can be simultaneously expanded, whereas in the brick and mortar world of storefronts and distributors, one must be sacrificed for the other. (Evans & Wurster pp. 30-31) The Internet has an inherent advantage in reach when comparing the number of people it reaches with the penetration of the direct market specialty store, or even adding in the bookstores. (Indeed, many smaller publishers look at the bookstores as an instance of increasing their reach beyond the direct market.) But web comics also frequently have an advantage in richness. While Marvel collects storyline in book format, in hopes to make it easier to find all parts of the story, a web comic will normally have its entire run online. Marvel, which had an early head start among the print publishers, initially used its dotComic format as a sort of stopgap measure between sold out issues and reprints made an attempt to use the web comic as a way of increasing richness. On the other hand, Crossgen, a company whose future is in some doubt due to financial problems, has perhaps the richest web comic site of all. After a six month embargo from the print release date, every comic they have published is online to be read. It is also the highest subscriber count for that economic model.

Evans & Wurster describe a three-way battle for consumers between suppliers, incumbent retailers and online stores (Evans & Wurster p. 100). This accurately describes the cannibalization fears and recriminations between publishers and retailers. Strangely, there seems not to be many pure Internet-based suppliers of print comics, with most of that business being snapped up by larger retailers who jumped on the bandwagon early, like the aforementioned Midtown Comics. Web comics tend not to suffer from these power struggles, as they sell directly to the consumers, what Evans and Wurster refer to throughout their book as "deconstructing the supply chain."

Blown to Bits is an extended meditation on the effects of reach and richness, and the deconstruction within. The main points are about market shifts, and it is necessary to delve a bit deeper into the peculiarities of the comic market to better address whether or not comics have been deconstructed or if a blow up is imminent.

Demographics could indicate if the audience is similar for print and web comics.

Crossgen	Dark Horse	Keenspot	Penny Arcade
93% Male (75%Age 14-24)	81% Male	Male: 77.2%	93.8% Male
7% Female (80% age 24-54)	19% Female	Female: 19.7%	Female: 5.6%
	Under 12: 5% 12 – 17: 26% 18-24: 37% 25-34: 24% 35-44: 4% 45-54:2% over 55: 1%	Under 18: 17% 18-24: 50.9% 25-30: 16.5% 31-35: 6.4% 36-40: 2.8% 41-50: 2.4% 51-60: 0.5% 61+: 0.3%	Under 18: 15.4% 18-24: 59.7% 24-34: 23.2% 35-44: 1.7% 45+: 0.2%
(Private Interview)	("Ads > Profile")	("Keenspot.com: Media Kit – Reader Demographics")	("Audience")

Indeed, the demographics do look similar, with print skewing slightly younger. There is a cross-over in video game interest between both formats and *Penny Arcade* includes the statistic that 28% of their readers regularly purchase comic books ("Audience").

If the demographic is the same, it has been established that the readership of web comics is much greater than print comics with *Penny Arcade*, alone, able to make a credible claim to having a larger readership than the combined patronage of the direct market and *Goats* having a readership that would put them as a borderline top 10 title. Perhaps a more drastic example would be the success of *BobandGeorge.com*. Bob and George is a homage to/satire of the Megaman video game. It gets 500,000 unique visitors each month and its creator, Dave Anez, makes a very, very conservative estimate of 25,000 to 30,000 regular readers. (Anez) In stark contrast, the *official* Megaman print comic book sold an estimated 9,750 copies in December 2003 ("Top 300 Comics Actual-- December 2003"). The online pastiche has, at worst, three times the reach and best 50 times the reach of the genuine article. Clearly something is amiss.

On the fiscal side, there are opportunities to experiment with new formats and genres online in smaller numbers than print will support. The more popular websites have demonstrated potential to earn equivalent revenue to an independent comic book. It is also true that, with one or two notable exceptions, a web comic does not yet seem able to compete with the creative budget of a mainstream publisher, such as Marvel. Web comics are also starting to sell printed editions online in similar numbers to direct market trade paperbacks.

Have web comics blown up print comics? Yes and no. The Marvels and DCs seem to be somewhat stable, if not where they were 10 years ago. The distribution system exists for their benefit, and they can take advantage of it. The threat of a blow-up looms, if the direct market should continue to shrink. Without the direct market and monthly comic books, trade paperback collections would become expensive to produce and there is some question how many of them would be profitable without being subsidized by their initial serialization. Web comics are a still a threat, but tend not to venture often into the superhero genre that the major comic book companies own.

Independent comics, however, do seem to have been blown up. There are few of them around, where once there was reasonable market share. The financial incentive to run first to print is not immediately clear. Web comics show fewer limitations to circulation than an independent print comic, and fewer independent print comics are popping up. Perhaps the strangest incentive is that while web comics have a similar income potential to a independent print comic book, the amount of material being produced in a month is often less, as web comics are often formatted in smaller pieces of art than a comic book page.

Chapter 9: Conclusions and Takeaways – Revisited and Revised

It is apparent that the print comic book industry, through its own policies and distribution networks, has limited its potential audience. Conversely, Web Comics are attracting audiences at, or in some cases above, the level of comic book readership in more stable times. Crossgen, in particular, was able to reach an audience over ten times the print circulation of an individual comic with their AOL Web Comic arrangement.

* Business Takeaway – You cannot compete with the Internet on the basis of reach. When distribution limitation in the brick and mortar world are an issue, the Internet is the quickest route to expansion.

Further, there is evidence to support the belief that the direct market in general, and Diamond Comics Distributors specifically, is operated in such a way as to give the more established companies, specifically Diamond's Premiere Partners, an inherent advantage. While this does work to the benefit of large publishers like Marvel and DC, it creates not so much of a barrier to entry, as a barrier to market share, for new and smaller publishers. The only recent start-up publishers enjoying any success being recent departures from Premiere Partner, Image Comics, only serves to reinforce the view that these Premiere Partners are the only way to gain retailer attention. Taken in the aggregate, this also means that the genres of print comics are tightly clustered around the superhero, with a few science fiction, horror and adventure titles scattered around the side. Contrast this with Web Comics, where humor, gaming and computer usage are dominant genres and the growing chasm between the audiences becomes more pronounced.

* Business Takeaway – Exclusivity contracts and placement are a bigger problem in the real world, than cyberspace. Yes, partnering with AOL or MSN can increase your traffic, profile and business. Ultimately, though, search engines, links and word of mouth are a powerful equalizer in this space.

Web Comics and Print Comics have started to compete in print form. *PVP* has a moderately successful black and white print edition under the Image imprint, but monthly (bi-monthly in the case *of PVP*) comic books are not the main point of direct competition, so much as the trade paperback. Interestingly, the most popular trade paperbacks reprinting Web Comics compete directly and comparably with trade paperbacks reprinting top Print Comics. MegaTokyo, in particular is a strong performer in the mainstream book trade, and Penny Arcade seems to move thousands of books directly off its site. Many other Web Comics have their reprints post similar numbers to smaller reprint collections from the Premiere Partners or good sellers from the smaller publishers, Girl Genius being an example of a solid mid-list title, despite originating the material online. This market is developing and will be interesting to watch in the future.

Fiscally, there are many revenue models to take into account when looking at Web Comics. Merchandising is the wild card among revenue models. Due to the idiosyncratic nature of comics, not all Web Comics are equally suited to merchandising. For those that are, it is by far the most lucrative documented revenue stream.

Micropayments and subscriptions are tools of economic efficiency. Much like the direct market for Print Comics makes the business model efficient by not accepting returns on unsold products, these two similar revenue streams make the usage of bandwidth efficient, only allowing the customer to view what they have paid for and charging a higher rate per view than would normally be accruable through advertising. Unfortunately, research indicates that only 1% of the natural online audience will pay for content if it has been freely available. This is where bandwidth enters the equation. Prices on bandwidth vary greatly, but it is generally accepted that there is a middle ground, between the entry level web hosting agreements and the large bulk user accounts where bandwidth becomes more expensive that banner advertising at the lower ad rates would be able to pay for. In the absence of a good merchandising program, which would need the extra 99% of potential traffic that a payment would drive away, micropayments and subscriptions have the potential to help grow a strip past that median level of popularity without incurring an operating loss. Subscriptions are better for ongoing content, while micropayments are suited for individual pieces. When dealing with a few million pageviews each month, advertising becomes a better way to go than micropayments, and the bandwidth price lowers enough in bulk for the model to right itself. Still, bandwidth prices drop every month and this increasingly becomes less and less of an issue.

An ideal revenue model will likely change for each Web Comic, but an optimum case, assuming the material is suitable, would be an advertising-based Web Comic with extensive merchandising, taking advantage of both revenue streams. For the purposes of this thesis, printed editions of Web Comics are considered a form of merchandising.

* Business Takeaway – Is the same. In a sense, when you monetize content on the web, you're always selling something: your own content in the case of subscriptions, micropayments, or donations; merchandise, be it your own or through an affiliate; and when you sell advertising on your site, you're ultimately facilitating the sale of someone else's product. Experiment and find out what kind of selling works best for your site. Expect to make more money if you can sell a physical product that's either an off-shoot of, or complimentary to, your content.

When comparing the revenue generated by Web and Print Comics, the trends of the direct market must be paid attention to and the drastic circulation difference between large and small publishers accounted for. While the largest of the Web Comics have revenue streams that might rival the creative budget of Marvel Comics, on the whole, web comics do not generate as much revenue as an issue from a major print publisher. Conversely, many Web Comics do generate equal or greater cash flow than their print cousins of the small and independent press. Scott McCloud is quick to point out while he hasn't made a huge amount of money off his micropayments, he likely would not have broken even attempting to print the same comic. It is a reasonable conclusion that unless a cartoonist is producing for a major Print Comics publisher, that cartoonist is better served building a web audience, particularly if the comic is not of the superhero genre, which still rules the direct market. At the same time, the Web Comics continue to grow in circulation and more may rival the mainstream print market in revenue, particularly if banner ad rates increase.

* Business Takeaway – Not every site is a full-time business with full-time profits. Many sites operate

profitably on a smaller scale. Know your market and grow your audience and client base. In the online world, the comparative lack of sunk costs, not the least being rent, makes it possible to show profits more quickly, especially on a cash-flow basis, and grow into something bigger.

To the question of whether Web Comics have caused Print Comics to be "blown to bits," the answer is partially. At this time, the major publishers, as defined as Diamond's Premiere Partners, are still healthy. Continued atrophy of the direct market could change that. It is generally agreed, however, that it is very difficult, if not impossible, to start a new Print Comics publisher. Web Comics have, to some degree, stepped in and are picking up large audiences as the printed small press continues to wither in circulation. Web Comics show greater diversification of genre. Web Comics are, at minimum, in the process of blowing up the Print Comics small press, if they have not already done so. Currently, it is already apparent that the revenue streams are comparable if not favorable and the trade paperback numbers similar. With the possibility of increased merchandising as an added bonus, Web Comics are making inroads and recruiting a similar demographic to Print Comics, but in greater numbers.

* Business Takeaway: The web affords a greater agility in business and opportunity to experiment with different audiences that while existing in large numbers as an aggregate, are too widely scattered to create a large physical presence in any one place. The web is an aggregator of niche markets. It is frequently the consolidator of "cult" markets. Look for opportunity by diversifying into different flavors of form and content, much as web comics have adopted niche themes to the comics medium.

Business on the Internet is constantly changing, and so are the corporate policies of the Print Comics publishers. The continued expansion into bookstores by Web Comics is a phenomenon to be carefully watched. Print Comics publishers, especially Marvel and DC, should they ever decide to make a serious attempt to enter the Web Comics market, could certainly alter the landscape of these issues. Similarly, various publishers must renew their contracts with Diamond, and the same structure that has benefited the top publishers is not guaranteed to exist in perpetuity. Micropayments are suddenly workable and the initial experiments have built on the efforts of subscriber-based sites with an increasing willingness for viewers to pay for online content. The question is no longer whether or not there is demand, merely how large the demand is. The banner ad market has bounced back for the moment. Print On Demand offers options for almost every strip to issue a collected print edition, if perhaps not a low enough production cost for all strips to go into commercial distribution.

The art form is now to mix the business streams. The largest question is for which markets, if any, will the paid download system work better than the freely-viewed merchandising and advertising system? This may partially boil down to what kind of merchandising options are natural for the property. Not all comics lend themselves equally to t-shirts and stuffed animals.

Publishers should be careful about falling in love with a merchandising model if they don't own the intellectual property.

Independent cartoonists should be careful about falling in love with the paid download model if they don't have a strong name or a publisher with enough brand equity to ascribe worth to a new artist.

More people continue to make a living publishing web comics. There is definitely money in the market. Ending up with a printed edition is increasingly the end product. Past that, it is up to the individual to mix and match revenue streams that match the property.

Bibliography

Abrams, Pete. The Sluggy Freelance Comic for Monday, August 25, 1997. 25 August 1997. www.sluggy.com. 14 Feb. 2004.
<http://www.sluggy.com/daily.php?date=970825>

Ads > Profile. March 2003. www.DarkHorse.com 29 Feb. 2004. <http://services.darkhorse.com/ads/profiles.php>

Allen, Todd. "Dot-Comics Lure New Readers." Chicago Tribune. 24 June 2002: 4:3.

Anez, Dave. "Re: Interview Request." E-mail to author. 10 Feb. 2004.

Audience. 4 November 2003. www.penny-arcade.com. 16 Feb. 2004. <http://www.penny-arcade.com/pamediakit/page_2.htm>

Bald Rocket Productions | Advertising - Sexy Losers. August 2003. "Hard" / Sexylosers.com. 16 Feb. 2004.
<http://baldrocket.com/ads/sexylosers.shtml>

Bookscan. Adult Fiction Overall Graphic Novels Week Ending: 12/31/03. 13 February 2004 newsarama.com 20 Feb. 2004.

Crosbie, Vin. "The 1% Solution?" Click Z. 8 October 2002.
<http://www.clickz.com/design/freefee/article.php/1477881>

Crosby, Chris. "Re: Gav sent me over." E-mail to author. 13 Feb. 2004.

Diamond. "Diamond's Terms & Conditions of Sale."
Update Unknown. www.diamondcomics.com 20 Feb.
2004.
<http://vendor.diamondcomics.com/vendor5.html#Sales
%20Minimums>

Diamond. "The Product Life Cycle." Update Unknown.
www.diamondcomics.com 20 Feb. 2004.
<http://vendor.diamondcomics.com/propterms.html>

Extreme Tracking – Bob and George. 16 February 2004.
Extreme Tracking. 16 Feb. 2004. <
http://extremetracking.com/open;unique?login=qtrelane>

Extreme Tracking – Sinfest. 16 February 2004. Extreme
Tracking. 16 Feb. 2004.
<http://extremetracking.com/open;sum?tag=musepimp>

Evans, Philip and Thomas S. Wurster. Blown to Bits.
Boston: Harvard Business School Press, 2000.

Frazier, J.D. UF – 1997 Cartoon Archive. Update
Unknown. www.userfriendly.org. 14 Feb. 2004. <
http://www.userfriendly.org/cartoons/archives/1997.htm
l>.

Godin, Seth. Unleashing the Idea Virus. Dobb's Ferry,
NY: Do You Zoom, Inc., 2000.

Hanson, Ward. Principles of Internet Marketing.
Cincinnati: South-Western College Publishing, 2000.

Hard. "Re: Interview Request." E-mail to author. 9 Feb.
2004.

Hibbs, Brian. "Tilting at Windmills v2 #2" 13 February 2004 www.newsarama.com 20. Feb. 2004

ICV2. "Top 300 Comics Actual--December 2003." 13 February 2004. www.icv2.com. 20 Feb. 2004. <http://www.icv2.com/articles/news/4107.html>

ICV2. "Top 50 Graphic Novels Actual--January 2004." 13 February 2004. www.icv2.com. 20 Feb. 2004. <http://www.icv2.com/articles/news/4263.html>

Jenkins, Henry. "Selling Online Content – 25 Cents at a Time." Technology Review 10 Sept 2003 http://www.technologyreview.com/articles/wo_jenkins09 1003.asp?p=0

Jenkins, Henry. "Will the Web Save Comics?." Technology Review 1 May 2002. <http://www.technologyreview.com/articles/wo_jenkins0 50102.asp>

Johnson, Drew. Goats: The Faq. 1 April 2002. www.Goats.com. 14 Feb. 2004. <http://goats.com/features/faq/>

Keenspot.com: Media Kit – Reader Demographics. Update Unknown. www.keenspot.com 29 Feb. 2004. < http://www.keenspot.com/mediakit/ratecard.html>

Keenspot.com: Media Kit – Rate Card. Update Unknown. www.keenspot.com 16 Feb. 2004. < http://www.keenspot.com/mediakit/ratecard.html>

Keenspot.com: Media Kit – What We Are. February 2004. www.keenspot.com 16 Feb. 2004. < http://www.keenspot.com/mediakit/index.html>

Khoo, Robert. "Re: Interview Request." E-mail to author. 10 Feb. 2004.

Kurtz, Scott. Become a PVP Sponsor. January 2003. Scott R. Kurtz. 16 Feb. 2004 <http://www.pvponline.com/metrics.php3>

Manley, Joey. "Re: Interview Request." E-mail to author. 10 Feb. 2004.

Miller, John Jackson, Maggie Thompson, Peter Bickford, and Brent Frankenhoff. The Standard Catalog of Comic Books – Second Edition. Iola, WI: Krause Publications, 2003.

Modahl, Mary. Now or never: how companies must change today to win the battle for Internet consumers. New York: HarperCollins, 2000.

Palmer, Jonathan W., and Lars Bo Eriksen. "Digital News: Content, Delivery, and Value Propositions for an Intangible Product." Journal of End User Computing 12.4 (2000): 11-19.

Parker, Charley. About Argon Zark. Update Unknown. www.zark.com. 14 Feb. 2004. < http://www.zark.com/front/about.html>

Rate Card. 4 November 2003. www.penny-arcade.com. 16 Feb. 2004. <http://www.penny-arcade.com/pamediakit/page_3.htm>

Real Life – Advertisers. 2004. RealLifeComics.com. 16 Feb. 2004. <http://www.reallifecomics.com/advertisers.php>

Richman, Dan. "Comics Publisher Fantagraphics Drawn into a Financial Crisis." 30 May 2003. Seattle Post-Intelligencer. 20 Feb. 2004.
<http://seattlepi.nwsource.com/business/124315_fantagraphic30.html>

San Giacomo, Mike. My Epic Postmortem. 14 November 2003. www.comicon.com 21 Feb. 2004.
<http://newsarama.com/forums/showthread.php?s=&threadid=6629>

Shirky, Clay. "Fame vs Fortune: Micropayments and Free Content." 5 Sept. 2003. "Networks, Economics and Culture.
<http://shirky.com/writings/fame_vs_fortune.html>.

Stevens, R. "Re: Interview Request." E-mail to author. 17 Feb. 2004.

The Advertising Page. Update Unknown. BobandGeorge.com 16 Feb. 2004
<http://www.bobandgeorge.com/Other/Advertise.html>

The Story Behind Kevin and Kell. 11 November 2003. Kevinandkell.com. 14 February 2004. < http://www.kevinandkell.com/about/index.html>.

Support MegaTokyo. Update Unknown. Megatokyo.com 21 Feb. 2004 <http://www.megatokyo.com/support.php>

UPS. Calculate Time and Cost. Custom Calculation. UPS.com. 21 Feb 2004.
<http://wwwapps.ups.com/ctc/packageInfo#listbox>

Value Web. "Red Hat Linux." Update Unknown.
www.valueweb.com 26 Feb. 2004
<http://www.valueweb.com/dedicated/dedicated-
servers/redhat.htm>

Vogel, Harold L.. Entertainment Industry Economics: A
Guide for Financial Analysis, 5th Edition. Cambridge:
Cambridge University Press, 2001.

What's New, September 1993. September. 1993.
University of Illinois, Champaign-Urbana. 14 Feb. 2004.
<http://shirky.com/writings/fame_vs_fortune.html>.

Zale, Peter. Helen, Sweetheart of the Internet. Update
Unkown. Peterzale.com. 14 Feb. 2004. <
http://www.peterzale.com/helen/>

Interviews

Jemas, Bill.   Chief Marketing Officer, Marvel
Entertainment. February 12, 2004.

Panaccio, Tony. Former Vice President of Product
Development, Crossgen Entertainment. February 10,
2004.

Printed in the United States
111341LV00005B/95/A